READER BONUS!

Dear Reader,

As a thank you for your support, Action Takers Publishing would like to offer you a special reader bonus: a free download of our course, "How to Write, Publish, Market & Monetize Your Book the Fast, Fun & Easy Way." This comprehensive course is designed to provide you with the tools and knowledge you need to bring your book to life and turn it into a successful venture.

The course typically **retails for $499**, but as a valued reader, you can access it for free. To claim your free download, simply follow this link ActionTakersPublishing.com/workshops - use the discount code "coursefree" to get a 100% discount and start writing your book today.

If we are still giving away this course by the time you're reading this book, head straight over to your computer and start the course now. It's absolutely free.

READER BONUS!

ActionTakersPublishing.com/workshops
discount code "coursefree"

*Stepping Out of Your Comfort Zone
to Achieve Massive Success*

BOLD
RISKS
BIG
REWARDS

Email: lynda@actiontakerspublishing.com

Website: www.actiontakerspublishing.com

ISBN # (paperback) 978-1-956665-54-3

ISBN # (Kindle) 978-1-956665-55-0

Published by Action Takers Publishing™

Table of Contents

*You can dream, hope, desire, want, manifest, and pray for
everything you want in life, but when it's staring you in
the face, Nothing Happens Without Action. Take action to
effect the change you wish to be and see in the world.*
~Lynda Sunshine West

Introduction

L ife is punctuated by moments of decision, where the path ahead forks into the safe and the unknown. More often than not, the allure of security and the comfort of the familiar beckon us, urging us to remain within the boundaries of what we know aka The Comfort Zone. But what lies beyond the edge of comfort? What potential could be unlocked by choosing the path less traveled? "Bold Risks, Big Rewards" invites you to explore these questions, presenting a compelling argument for embracing the unknown as a gateway to extraordinary possibilities.

In these pages, you will encounter stories of ordinary people who made extraordinary decisions. These aren't just tales of success but are honest narratives encompassing fear, failure, and fortitude. They reveal the simple truth that the road to achievement is often paved with setbacks. Yet, it is precisely these challenges that carve the contours of character and crystallize the essence of achievement.

"Bold Risks, Big Rewards" is not merely a collection of success stories; it is a manifesto for living courageously. Each chapter invites you to explore different aspects of risk-taking—from career leaps and personal ventures to emotional and financial gambles. The individuals you will meet in this book faced their fears head-on, armed with nothing but a conviction to pursue what felt right, even when it wasn't easy or assured. Their journeys illuminate the profound impact of stepping beyond the safety net, embracing the potential for failure as much as success.

This book also serves as a mirror, reflecting back not just stories, but the lessons embedded within them. You'll learn that risk-taking is a dynamic process of self-exploration, asking us to constantly reassess our boundaries and push beyond them. It teaches us about resilience— the kind that is forged in the fires of uncertainty and quenched in the waters of new beginnings. Through these stories, you will discover that the essence of risk-taking lies not in reckless abandon, but in calculated courage, a balance between the fear of failure and the thrill of possibility.

As you turn each page, allow the stories encourage you to reflect on your own life's crossroads. Where have you held back for fear of failure or fear of success? What dreams have you set aside for the illusion of safety? "Bold Risks, Big Rewards" challenges you to rethink these decisions, to consider what might be possible if you dared to venture beyond the proverbial comfort zone (after all, the comfort zone is oftentimes not a comfortable place to be).

By the end of this book, you will understand that the most profound rewards often come from the boldest risks. These are the rewards that enrich not just our bank accounts but our very souls, gifting us with growth, wisdom, and fulfillment that security could never offer. This book doesn't just invite you to take risks; it invites you to redefine what it means to live fully.

Embrace the lessons within "Bold Risks, Big Rewards." Allow them to move you, challenge you, and inspire you to embark on your own journey of risk and reward. The question isn't whether you will encounter fear, but whether you will greet it as a barrier or as a gateway to a life of richness and authenticity. Remember, on the other side of risk, not just success awaits, but a greater version of yourself, refined by the trials and triumphs of daring greatly.

Are you ready to take the leap? The rewards promise to be nothing short of transformative.

What risk will you take today?

Lynda Sunshine West and Sally Larkin Green

CHAPTER 1

The Leap Into Legacy

Lynda Sunshine West

This chapter is dedicated to those who are working in the corporate world and want to make the leap into entrepreneurship. If it were easy, everyone would be doing it. It's well worth the leap, if you feel inclined to do so.

The Corporate Labyrinth: 36 Years, 49 Jobs

"I'm convinced that about half of what separates the successful entrepreneurs from the non-successful ones is pure perseverance." ~Steve Jobs

---

If you knew without a doubt that you would be successful as an entrepreneur and not have to worry about money or health insurance, would you take the leap from your 9 to 5 and test yourself?

In 2020, Global Entrepreneurship Monitor did a study and discovered that about 37% of entrepreneurs in the United States were engaged in some form of hybrid entrepreneurship (part entrepreneur/ part employee). This approach allows individuals to test their business ideas, build a customer base, and ensure a steady income before transitioning to full-time entrepreneurship.

As an employee for 36 years at 49 jobs, I had my fair share of working for "the man."

I started off working at the local county fair at age 16. I made cotton candy by day and shoveled poop by night (don't worry, I did wash my hands in between). My introduction into the working world was working two jobs. I loved the freedom of being able to buy the clothes I wanted to buy without anyone telling me what I could or couldn't wear. Those first two jobs were my steppingstones into freedom and led to my next job at age 17 working at a yummy fast food burger place called Carl's Jr.

After high school, I decided to work as a bank teller. So I went to school and, immediately after finishing school, got hired at a credit union. I was only 19 and was working as a bank teller supervisor, supervising 12 tellers.

I didn't know it at the time, but I must have been pretty darn good to be so young as a supervisor. I'll take a moment to pat myself on the back right now.

SIDE NOTE: I don't think we give ourselves enough credit for what we do, and I think we need to frequently stop what we're doing to pat ourselves on the back. Go ahead. Stop reading (but come back here) and think of something you're proud of yourself for and literally pat yourself on the back.

I only worked on that job for 18 months (the longest I ever stayed at one job) because I was working 75 hours per week and, as a single mom, had two babies at home (4 weeks and 14 months) who called the babysitter "Mommy." That tore at my soul. I was a young mother who did what she needed to do to put food on the table, but I wasn't raising my kids, a stranger was. I ended up meeting an awesome man when I was 25 (I call him Wheatie) and three years later we were married. The four of us lived a good life together. I finally had the right father for my kids.

Those 49 jobs led to me learning new computer programs, new ways of doing things, training every new employee who came to every job. I had a lot of responsibility, but I never climbed the corporate ladder (I wasn't anywhere long enough).

I'm not gonna bore you with all of my jobs; however, I will share that my 49th job was working for a judge in the Ninth Circuit Court of Appeals. I made it. The penultimate. I climbed the corporate ladder, but not within one company. Instead, I climbed it in one position, legal secretary.

Job = Freedom? I don't know about that.

In the structured world of corporate jobs, many individuals find themselves navigating a labyrinth of strict schedules, rigid hierarchies, and repetitive tasks that can feel suffocating over time. The promise of stability often comes at the cost of creativity and personal growth, as employees are pushed to conform to predefined roles and expectations that leave little room for innovation or deviation. The daily grind can stifle one's passions and mute their aspirations, turning the pursuit of career advancement into a monotonous quest for incremental gains. The corporate setting can start to feel like a cage and you're the one inside clawing to get out. You start to weigh your options, job security or personal and professional freedom that entrepreneurship can provide.

I felt like a caged animal watching the world around me. I felt deep down inside of me that there was more to life than what I was doing, but I didn't know what.

I remember it as if it were yesterday. It was August of 2014. I was driving to the courthouse for work and had a feeling come across me. You know, that feeling in the pit of your stomach that something is wrong? I was stuck in traffic (as I had been for 36 years), but something was different that day. I was overwhelmed with dread. My stomach was queasy, my palms were sweaty, anger was making its way to the top of my head and I felt like I was gonna blow my top.

I started pounding on the steering wheel and yelling at the top of my lungs, "Why am I here? What's the purpose of this planet? Why are we ALL here? As a matter of fact, what is MY purpose? I have no value. I have no purpose. I have no reason to be here."

Then I drove the next 20 minutes in that traffic, filled with anger and hate. I hated my job. I hated my life. Even though I love my husband, that wasn't enough. I felt a deep desire for more. I got to work, walked into the judge's chambers, and got on my computer to start my Groundhog Day life.

When I logged onto Facebook (we weren't permitted to do so, but I was so bored I did it anyway) there was a post inside of a group from a woman named Liz Stone.

"Hi ladies. I'm a life coach. I took some time off and am getting back into it. I'm looking for five women who want to change their lives. Is that you?"

Her post spoke directly to me. I ended up working with her as my life coach for the most pivotal five months ever. After working with Liz, I had a huge epiphany. My realization was that I had a lot of fears and I allowed my fears to stop me from living.

That was when I decided to take the leap into entrepreneurship. I quit my cushy corporate job working for the judge and became an entrepreneur. That was also when I decided to break through one fear every day for an entire year aka The Year of Fears.

Embracing the Entrepreneurial Spirit: The First Leap

I don't have time to go into my whole entrepreneurial journey, but I will tell you this: It's been both the scariest and most rewarding thing I've ever done in my life. The ups and downs, twists and turns, forward and backward moments come and go, but there's always one thing that keeps me going: my burning desire to do and be so much more. Every story I've experienced along my journey has led me to becoming a book publishing expert.

I jumped into the entrepreneurial world without a net. If I could turn back time, I would do some things differently, but I have no regrets about the way I did do things. I needed every step in order to have the growth I have had after leaving the stifling corporate world that didn't train me to be independent; rather, it readied me to become reliant on my employers to provide for me.

The Call to Publish: Discovering My True Calling

Shortly after becoming an entrepreneur, I was invited to share my story in a collaboration book titled, *Footsteps of the Fearless*. Since I was breaking through one fear every day that year, it made sense for me to join a book about fearlessness. I raised my hand and said, "Yes, I'm in." That was the catalyst for me becoming a book publisher.

After being part of that book, I wrote a book titled, *The Year of Fears*, where I share my journey of breaking through a fear every day for a year.

After *The Year of Fears*, I decided to follow in my mentor's footsteps and put together a collaboration book titled, *Momentum: 13 Lessons from Action Takers Who Changed the World*. I wasn't aware of what was to come, but that step was another pivotal moment in my life. That was the start of what would become Action Takers Publishing.

Legacy and Impact: Envisioning the Future

Our mission at Action Takers Publishing is to empower 5 million women and men to share their stories with the world to make a greater impact on the planet. I found that sharing my story was not only healing for me, but was also impactful for those who heard it.

Have you ever read or heard a story that was transformative for you? Yes or no? If yes, I want you to think of it this way. If someone else's story transformed your life, is it all possible that YOUR story can be that transformation for someone else?

Yes, 100%.

That's why I encourage everyone to share their story. Storytelling has been around since the beginning of time. Your story matters. There are people who need to hear it because your story will make a difference in their lives.

If you haven't yet written your story, sit down and start now. There's no time like the present because the future is never promised. Take a bold risk of putting yourself out there in the world to shine your bright light and reap the rewards that are awaiting you.

Lynda Sunshine West

She ran away at 5 years old and was gone an entire week, came home riddled with fears and, in turn, became a people-pleaser.

At age 51, she decided to break through one fear every day for a year and, in doing so, she gained an exorbitant amount of confidence to share her story. Her mission is to empower 5 million women and men to write their stories to make a greater impact on the planet.

Lynda Sunshine West is the Founder and CEO of Action Takers Publishing, a Bestseller Book Publishing Expert, Speaker, 38 Times #1 International Bestselling Author, Former Contributing Writer at Entrepreneur Magazine, Senior Level Executive Contributing Writer at Brainz Magazine, and Executive Film Producer.

Connect with Lynda Sunshine at https://www.actiontakerspublishing.com/lynda.

CHAPTER 2

Runaway Hearts

Sally Larkin Green

To my four brothers, Ricky, Darren, Jimmy, and
Christopher. Love, your big sister!

In the spring of 1962, Florence, or Ossie as she was nicknamed, and Richie, two high school sweethearts, found themselves on the brink of a life-altering decision. Bound by love and a secret they could no longer keep hidden, they planned to run away. It was a decision they believed would lead them to a new beginning.

Richie was the kind of boy who was both athletic and handy. Florence, with her quick wit and boundless creativity, complemented him perfectly. They were inseparable, but as they neared the end of his senior year, an unexpected twist in their story emerged—Ossie was pregnant!

The news made them pause, filling them with fear and uncertainty. They knew their parents would never understand or forgive them easily. After a tear-filled conversation, they made a decision that felt like their only hope—they would run away to Maryland and elope. They had heard that in Maryland they could get married without needing their parents' permission.

Packing their bags with trembling hands and determined hearts, they left notes for their families and convinced Richie's twin sister to drive them to the train station. The train ride to Maryland was a whirlwind of mixed emotions—excitement for the life they envisioned and anxiety about the unknown.

They stepped off the train onto unfamiliar grounds, their hearts pounding in unison. Grabbing each other's hands, they hailed a cab. "Take us to a Justice of the Peace, please," Richie said to the cab driver, a middle-aged man with kind eyes who noticed the nervous glances between the young couple.

As they drove through the streets of Maryland, the driver watched the couple in his rearview mirror. "You two running away?," he asked, half in jest, half in concern.

Richie's confident nod no did little to mask the driver's underlying worry. The cab driver, sensing there was more to the story than what was shared, made a decision that would alter their course once again. Instead of heading to the Justice of the Peace, he pulled into the local police station.

"What's going on?," Ossie asked as they were ushered inside.

"We're just making sure everything's alright," the cab driver said, his voice a mix of apology and firmness.

The police were kind but firm. They listened to Ossie and Richie's story and gently explained that they needed to call their parents. A phone call that was a mix of tears, relief, and stern instructions to come home immediately.

Stranded without money and feeling the heavy weight of their youthful naivety, Richie took off his watch—and hocked it. It was enough money to secure them a night's stay and two tickets home on the next train.

That night, they held each other close, their dreams bruised but not broken. They spoke of the future, of the child they would raise together, and the life they would build, no matter the obstacles.

The morning train ride back to Bridgeport was quiet, a relief from the whirlwind of emotions Ossie and Richie had experienced over the last 24 hours. As the landscape whizzed by, each tree and building inching them closer to their reality, they rehearsed what they would say to their parents. They were prepared for disappointment and anger, but above all, they hoped for understanding and support.

Arriving back in their hometown, the air felt different, heavier somehow. At the train station was a crowd of both parents and siblings. Richie had five siblings and Ossie had eight. Richie's parents were the first to greet them at the station, their expressions a complex tapestry of relief and disapproval. Ossie's parents followed, more subdued. They had made arrangements for them to get married that afternoon at the local church. It was April 16, 1962.

Eight months later, Ossie and Richie welcomed their daughter into the world. They named her Sally, a name filled with hope and a promise of new beginnings. Sally's arrival seemed to mend the fractures within their families, binding them with new ties and shared love.

Ossie and Richie took a bold risk that day, a risk that set the foundation for their journey together. They lived a life filled with challenges and profound joys. Sally was the first of their five children. The family they created became the ultimate reward for their commitment and determination.

Over the next 60 years, their marriage was a testament to resilience and unwavering love. They faced countless ups and downs, from the chaos of raising a large family to personal setbacks that tested their relationship. There were times of struggle and heartache in their lives, but also times of laughter and shared dreams that strengthened their bond.

Throughout the years, Richie remained the kind of man who could fix and build anything, not just with his hands, but with his heart. Ossie, his steadfast partner, brought warmth and grace to their home, nurturing their family with love and creativity. Together, they built a life that was rich in memories and full of enduring love.

Today, Richie cares for Ossie, who now battles Alzheimer's, with the same dedication and tenderness that marked their early years. His daily acts of care and compassion reflect a love that has only deepened with time.

Though their journey has been far from easy, Ossie and Richie have shown that true love can endure all things. Their story is a reminder that love is not just about the good times, but about standing by each other through every challenge. In the end, their unwavering commitment to each other proves that love wins, shining brightly through every chapter of our lives.

As I reflect on my parents' decision to run away and elope upon discovering my mother's being pregnant with me, I am filled with a deep sense of gratitude and admiration for their courage and love. Growing up, the stories of their attempted elopement were a cherished part of my family's story. My aunts and uncles would often talk about it, and my dad, with a twinkle in his eye, would say, "You know, Sally was there." As a child, their stories made me feel as if my existence was intertwined with their grand, romantic adventure. It was a source of pride and joy and solidified my belief in the power of love.

My parents' marriage, which has lasted over 60 years, is a testament to their devotion to each other and our family. It hasn't always been easy. My dad sometimes drove me crazy, but his love and devotion to my mom and our family never wavered. I have always admired their resilience and the love that carried them through both good times and bad. This has instilled in me a belief that true love is worth fighting for and that marriage requires both sacrifice and patience.

Knowing that "I" was the reason for their bold move made me feel there was a special purpose for my existence. This sense of purpose has driven me to pursue my dreams with passion and determination. I've always felt that there must be a reason God placed me on this earth, and this belief has motivated me to go after things I might not have otherwise pursued.

As I grew older, I came to understand the societal stigma associated with being pregnant before marriage. It wasn't until adulthood that I fully grasped the bravery required for my parents to defy those norms. By then, I didn't care what people thought; I admired my parents for taking that bold risk.

Sally Larkin Green

Sally Larkin Green is the Vice President of Author Development at Action Takers Publishing. With a background in business, Sally's passion for storytelling and empowering others has transformed her into a bestselling author and inspirational speaker.

As Vice President of Author Development, Sally works with aspiring writers, guiding them and transforming their ideas into bestselling books. She provides invaluable feedback, accountability, and encouragement.

Beyond her publishing role, Sally is a sought-after inspirational speaker, sharing her experiences and insights. She is a multiple times bestselling author and has written two children's books.

Connect with Sally at www.actiontakerspublishing.com.

CHAPTER 3

Choosing Compassion Amid Chaos

Bridgetti Lim Banda

To my husband Roderick, whose unwavering support sustains me through every twist and turn of life's journey, even when my choices may seem irrational. Your love and encouragement are my anchor in the stormy seas of uncertainty.

To my sons Turyn and Justyn, who fill my heart with boundless love and pride.
Justyn, my dear son, your presence on that fateful day reminds me of the strength and courage that reside within us all. You are my inspiration, my joy, and my greatest blessing.

Turyn, my quiet anchor, your gentle presence brings peace to my soul. Your love for messing with my hair and your boundless hugs, even as an adult, are cherished reminders of the depth of your affection. You are a steady beacon of light in my life, and I am forever grateful for you.

With all my love and gratitude

B ridgetti Lim Banda recounts a fateful morning when a routine school drop-off became a pivotal moment of decision-making. Witnessing a car accident, Bridgetti acted swiftly to assist a distressed mother and her special needs daughter. Through her narrative, she explores the profound impact of split-second choices and the enduring value of compassion in the face of adversity. Reflecting on the interconnectedness of personal responsibility and altruism, Bridgetti invites readers to contemplate the bold risks and profound rewards inherent in acts of kindness.

It was just another morning of craziness getting children ready for school. If you are a parent, you know exactly what that looks like. Finally, we were ready to leave. I was dropping off my youngest at school, and as I was about to turn the corner at the traffic light, it turned red. Out of nowhere, a car rushed across the intersection, colliding with the car facing me. Thankfully, the car was not a total wreck, and for just a moment, I looked into the car and saw what looked like a mom in the driver's seat and a young lady in the passenger seat. Nothing unusual there, except I noticed the young lady in the passenger seat rocking back and forth.

As soon as it was safe, I turned the corner and stopped my car. I flagged down another car with a child wearing the same uniform my son was wearing for school and asked if they would drop my son off at school. He was horrified, but after giving him a hug and assuring him that he would be okay, he agreed. I made a quick call to the school to inform them that my son was being dropped off by another parent as I hurried towards the car with the young lady still rocking back and forth in the driver's seat. By this time, the ambulance and other services were on the scene.

The young lady wasn't going anywhere. She kept rocking. I gave her a hug and asked if she would mind helping me take care of her mum. She liked the idea and agreed to get into the ambulance. She would not let them touch her, so I asked if she could demonstrate to her mum how they would take care of her and show her how a neck brace should be worn. She agreed and allowed the ambulance team to put on a neck brace, but she wasn't going anywhere because she needed to get to work. I told her that her mum needed to go to the hospital and that she needed to hold her mum's hand so her mum would not feel afraid, allowing the doctors to take a proper look. She agreed but only if I could ride in the ambulance with her. I explained that I had my own car and that there was not enough space in the ambulance. So I asked her if it would be okay for me to drive my own car there, and we could see who got to the hospital first, assuring her that I would be right there with her.

I called the school again to make sure my son was okay and in his class. The school was only a very short drive away from the scene of the accident.

I drove along and was ready for the young lady as they disembarked from the ambulance. We went inside and I stayed at her side. Her mom went to one room, and she went to another. At this point, the staff realized that I was her support system and allowed me to hold her hand while they made sure she was okay. Thankfully, they were both okay, with no serious injuries other than whiplash. At this point, I knew we'd be friends. After they got the all-clear and mother and daughter were reunited, I gave them both a hug and shared my contact details and left.

Meanwhile, back at school, I had an anxious son feeling like his mother had just abandoned him to strangers. (I recently learned how that made my son feel, now that he is a parent to my beautiful grandchildren whom I adore and love with my whole heart and soul as much as I love my boys.) I soon got a call from the mom to invite me to lunch with her daughter. I was delighted to meet them under much better circumstances. It turns out the young lady, as I suspected, had special needs, and the reason I made that split-second decision to stop my car, entrust my baby with strangers, and help this mom and her daughter in distress.

It turns out that they were on their way to a place that employs people with special needs that morning when the accident occurred, and the reason the young lady was so upset was that she did not want to miss going to work that day because she would be letting her co-workers down. This was just one of many meet ups, some organized and some accidental in town, but I was always met with the biggest smile and the biggest of hugs whenever we would meet.

Over the years, as a first responder, I have often felt compelled to stop and help if I was first on the scene. But this particular incident would remain firmly etched in my mind always.

Sometimes we have to act quickly and make bold choices. I love my son with my whole soul, heart, and mind and would do anything for him as I would for his children. Decisions we make may seem to those who don't understand as a lack of love and compassion for those closest to us. But nothing I ever do has not been thought through even if just for a split second. Sometimes we need to make bold choices and be prepared to live with the consequences. My son has carried the insecurity of my choice in that moment, but he also knows that I love and care for him. Not a day went by without me telling my boys how much I love them and always will. This was one of many times I would stop at the side of the road to help a stranger in need without any exception or expectation.

Does it mean I love or care for my own family less? You decide. Does it mean I will do it again? Yes, in a heartbeat. Does it mean I am willing to endanger my life? Perhaps! It's all a perspective. As I stood amidst the chaos of the accident scene, time seemed to both stand still and rush by in a blur of urgency. In that moment, I was suddenly aware of the fragility of life and the unexpected twists it can take. It was a reminder that every decision, no matter how seemingly insignificant, can have profound consequences. Little did I know, this experience would not only test my resolve in the face of adversity but also lead me to confront the invisible battles I fight everyday – battles born from a split-second decision made in my youth that forever altered the course of my life. From a fractured relationship with my parents to the consequences of a jump from a roof at 12, leading to a life with chronic pain and debilitating diseases, my journey has been marked by challenges that few can fully comprehend. Yet it's through these struggles that I discovered the true power of compassion and resilience. Despite the confusion from those closest to me, I find comfort and purpose in helping others, knowing that every act of kindness brings light to both their lives and mine.

Perhaps helping others when I feel let down by those I feel should have cared for me is a coping mechanism, but one thing I know for sure is that helping others helps me maintain my sanity. It leaves me with less time to focus on myself, less I should lose myself and my mind in the process. I can do less now than when I was younger. Age and the progression of disease, particularly life with unseen diseases and its debilitating effect, can make you feel like you have no purpose and want to give up on life. Serving others when and while I can leaves me with less time and room for feeling sorry for myself. In a weird way, my unseen disabilities have saved me from myself. Am I bold? You decide.

This accident taught me several valuable lessons:

Firstly, trust your instincts: Had I not trusted my gut feeling that day, I might not have stopped my car and helped them. Sometimes we must take a leap of faith and trust our intuition to guide us in the right direction.

Secondly, empathy and compassion can break barriers: Despite the chaos and panic of the accident, I saw a person in need and instinctively wanted to help. By showing empathy and compassion, I could connect with the young lady and help her through a challenging situation.

Thirdly, the importance of support: By offering support and staying with them throughout the ordeal, I showed to them and to myself that even strangers can be a source of comfort and strength in difficult times.

My experience that day further reinforced my belief in choosing compassion amid chaos. It solidified the notion that bold risks can lead to big rewards – in this case, the reward of forging new friendships and helping others when they need it most.

Since then, I've continued to prioritise compassion and empathy in my life, seeking opportunities to help others whenever possible. Through this experience, I've learned that the true reward lies not in recognition or accolades, but in the knowledge that we've made a difference in someone else's life.

In conclusion, "Choosing Compassion Amid Chaos" has become more than just a chapter title for me. It's a guiding principle that shapes my actions and inspires me to take bold risks, even when the outcome is uncertain. I hope my story encourages you to embrace empathy, kindness, and compassion, even in the face of adversity and chaos. After all, it's through these bold choices that we can create meaningful connections and make the world a kinder place for everyone.

Bridgetti Lim Banda

Bridgetti Lim Banda is more than a Livestream Producer; she's a versatile professional.

In addition to her role as an Amazon Live Influencer, Number 1 bestselling Amazon Author, Global Goodwill Ambassador, and Invisible Disabilities Advocate, Bridgetti offers a wealth of expertise to the livestreaming landscape.

As the Founder and Executive Producer at B Live Media, she provides Livestreaming and Live Shopping as a Service (Laas). Beyond her technical responsibilities, Bridgetti takes on the role of a Talk Show Host, recognised for her talent in crafting signature introductions that artfully present the best version of guests before they even start speaking. Several guests have commented on her well-crafted questions and engaging interviewing skills, particularly when interviewing authors.

Connect with Bridgetti at www.blivemedia.com.

CHAPTER 4

Embracing Bold Risks: The Path to Greater Success

Dara Bose

In life, we often face crucial decisions that can either propel us forward or keep us stagnant. At the heart of these decisions lies the choice between playing it safe or taking bold risks. As someone who has navigated through numerous challenges and triumphs, I firmly believe that embracing bold risks is the key to unlocking greater success and fulfillment.

One of the most significant risks I've taken was writing my book, *You Are Meant for More: Finding Your Passion in God's Purpose*. It was a journey filled with raw vulnerability, where I shared my stories of trauma, failure, and my own battle with mental illness. The decision to lay bare my experiences to the world was nothing short of terrifying. The fear of judgment and criticism loomed large, but deep down, I knew it was a risk worth taking.

As I poured my heart and soul into the pages of my book, I grappled with doubts and insecurities. Would anyone resonate with my story? Would they understand the struggles I've faced? Despite the uncertainty, I pressed on, driven by a deep sense of purpose and a desire to make a difference in the lives of others.

The moment of truth came when my book was finally published. It was a culmination of years of hard work, perseverance, and unwavering faith. Yet, as the book hit the shelves, I couldn't help but feel a sense of trepidation. Would it be well-received, or would it fade into obscurity?

To my surprise and immense gratitude, the response was overwhelmingly positive. Women from all walks of life reached out to me, sharing how my book had touched their hearts and transformed their perspectives. They spoke of feeling heard and understood, of realizing that they were not alone in their struggles. It was a humbling experience, one that reaffirmed the power of vulnerability and the importance of taking bold risks.

Through my book, I learned that embracing bold risks is not just about seeking personal gain; it's about making a meaningful impact in the lives of others. It's about stepping out of our comfort zones and sharing our authentic selves with the world, knowing that our stories have the power to inspire, uplift, and empower.

But taking bold risks goes beyond just sharing our stories; it's about seizing opportunities, pursuing our passions, and embracing the unknown. It's about taking that leap of faith, even when the outcome is uncertain, trusting that the journey itself is worth it.

In my book, I explore the concept of failure and the fear that often holds us back from pursuing our dreams. I share personal anecdotes of setbacks and challenges, illustrating how each failure ultimately paved the way for growth and resilience. It's a reminder that failure is not the end of the road but a steppingstone to success.

Moreover, I delve into the transformative power of mindset and the importance of cultivating a positive outlook on life. Drawing from biblical wisdom and personal experiences, I offer insights on how shifting our perspective can lead to greater opportunities and blessings.

Ultimately, the message is clear: taking calculated risks leads to greater success than playing it safe. It's about daring to dream big, embracing uncertainty, and trusting in the journey. As I reflect on my own experiences, I'm reminded of these words:

"Life is either a daring adventure or nothing at all."
~Helen Keller

So, to all those standing at the crossroads of fear and possibility, I urge you to choose courage. Take that bold risk, chase that dream, and believe in the power of your story. For it is in the daring that we truly discover the depths of our potential and the richness of life's blessings.

As I continue on my journey, I am filled with gratitude for the risks I've taken and the lessons I've learned along the way. And while the path ahead may be uncertain, I walk forward with confidence, knowing that every bold risk is a step closer to the extraordinary life we are meant to live.

Where would you like to begin your journey of embracing bold risks?

Because... you are meant for more!

Dara Bose

Dara Bose is a certified NLP Practitioner, Life Coach, #1 International Best-Selling Author, and public speaker. She has spent years working on personal development while reaching top rankings in the multilevel marketing (MLM) industry. Through her work in MLM, she discovered her passion for building up other women and her purpose to help them thrive. The wife of a firefighter/paramedic and mother of three, Dara never ceases to amaze with finding time to support and uplift women in her community.

Whether through participating in small groups at church, organizing fundraising events, and everything in between, Dara represents her best self in all she does. She motivates women to seek their own selves through self-reflection, motivation, and friendship. Women seek out Dara for guidance regularly when working through difficult times, or just needing the support of another woman, mother, wife, or business owner. Constantly seeking to better herself and provide the best support she can to others, you can always find her reading a book or attending seminars that build her up and better equip her to share her messaging.

Dara is best known for the saying she uses regularly with her children and friends, which can be applied to anyone in most situations: "But did you die?" Most importantly, Dara wants all women to know, "You are worthy, you are beautiful, and you are meant for more."

Connect with Dara at www.darabose.com.

CHAPTER 5

A Surprising and Wonderful Road

Erin Brophey

To my Mom and Dad, my siblings and my children.
I love you!

I'll never forget the burning sensation in my eyes, on my skin, the uncontrollable tears streaming down my face, as I walked through mandatory gas chamber training at Army ROTC camp in Fort Lewis, Washington. As the many sensations flooded my mind, body and soul, I recall thinking "What did I get myself into?"

I grew up mostly in North Canton, Ohio, up to the age of 18, through the end of high school. I was the youngest child of four siblings. All four of my older siblings went to college at Miami University in Oxford, Ohio. I recall visiting them there with my mom and dad, whether we were moving them in or out or just visiting for Family Weekend or Little Sibs Weekend. I have such fond memories of visiting my siblings there and learning a bit firsthand what it was like to be in college. Exciting, thrilling, nerve wracking at times, but overall absolutely positive family memories.

When it was my turn to think about where, how or if I should attend college during my junior year of high school, my parents suggested I also go to Miami University in Ohio. We all grew up in Ohio; it was home. My parents were quick to point out that since it was in-state tuition, we were as a family prepared and able to afford the tuition. For some reason, that thought didn't feel right to me. It didn't sit well. I knew logically Miami is a wonderful college. I knew my older siblings thrived there. They enjoyed it and learned so much. They also had fun and mostly very positive experiences. Since I visited so many times while growing up, it felt a little boring. I felt like I had already experienced it in some ways (albeit I was in elementary school, or junior high or high school when I visited and not an actual college student).

I felt an unexplainable need and desire to choose a different path. I wanted to do something unique. I felt a calling to try something more adventurous, maybe a little scary, that would challenge me. I couldn't quite express the solution at the time, but I started attending various college presentations being held either at school or in our community. I came across a group of recruiters holding an information session about the University of Pennsylvania in Philadelphia, Pennsylvania. It sounded a bit scary, a bit out of my league, but I was intrigued. It was definitely not comfortable or boring. I did some research and discovered that tuition was about $60,000 a year (compared to $13,000 a year for Miami of Ohio (and most colleges in Ohio)).

I let me parents know my thought and my desire to apply to U Penn. Their first reaction was "Absolutely not!" Our little girl is not going to live in West Philadelphia, across the United States from our home!" Of course I was thinking "It's only one state away; that's not a big deal."

Lo and behold, my parents and I continued to argue about it for months. Finally, I convinced my dad to just let me visit. I asked if he would take me on a campus visit so we both could learn more. I vividly remember him telling me not to say hello to random strangers in the elevator or on the sidewalk as we toured campus. He said, "You're not Ohio anymore; everyone isn't as friendly as you."

As we toured around campus, visiting classrooms, dorms, cafeterias, I fell in love with it! I loved how all the people were so diverse. From differing religions, differing cultures, differing styles of dress and styles of communication. It felt exhilarating, fun and exactly the type of challenge I was looking for. I think my dad was hoping I'd hate it, that I'd feel it was too different and out of my comfort zone. Surprise, surprise I knew that's where I wanted to attend college.

Then it became an issue of cost/tuition. My dad said, "Find a way to pay for it and you can go."

I recalled an alumnus from our high school visiting our government class and she told us about her experience doing Navy ROTC at the University of Notre Dame. The light bulb clicked and I knew I could earn a scholarship. In the meantime, I worked on and applied to several colleges in Ohio and a few out of state in Michigan, Pennsylvania, New York and Maryland.

A few months later, I found out I got accepted to almost all the schools. I was still most excited about U Penn. I also found out that I was awarded a 4-year Army ROTC scholarship that would pay for all tuition, room and board to any college that had an Army ROTC program. I think my parents were hoping I'd change my mind after visiting many campuses and doing research. I let them know I received a full scholarship and I still wanted to go to Penn. Again, my parents said no. I was so frustrated and devastated. I took off to go for a run around our neighborhood to cool off. I sprinted to my big brother Tim's house about 15 minutes away. He is nine years older than me. He and his wife, Cindi, got married soon after he finished college at Miami and they now lived nearby and were working full time.

I got to Tim's house, banged on the front door fighting back the tears that were filling my eyes. I filled him in on what had transpired. I let him know I really wanted to go to Penn, using the Army ROTC scholarship. To hold my spot in the class, I had to send in the acceptance of the spot along with a $500 check. Well, I didn't even have my own bank account yet, let alone any of my own money!

Tim said, "Are you sure this is what you want to do?" I said, "Yes, I'm 100% positive." He pulled out his checkbook, wrote a $500 check to U Pen and gave it to me. Still sniffling and crying a bit, I thanked him and said, "But how?" He offered, "You just send this into Penn by the deadline and keep up with your schoolwork. I'll take care of Mom and Dad."

And so it was! I mailed in my acceptance, continued to work hard getting good grades, etc. To my surprise, Mom and Dad came around and eventually were so very excited for me and proud. When it came time to pack for Penn, pack for Army training, I was pumped and ready to go and was gushing with gratitude. I was filled with the sense of honor and pride one feels when serving in the military.

I wasn't exactly sure what or why I was drawn to want to pursue Penn and the US Army, but I do know I had and have Guardian Angels and God all around me and with me continually leading my way.

Through the experience, I learned how to lead others to help them achieve their goals and dreams also. People in our lives want to protect us and it sometimes holds us back. They want the best for us. I've learned to always follow the little voice in my head and to follow the little signs that pop up in life.

We can't see the entire path into the future, but keep moving forward and the path will become clear. I am grateful, proud and honored to be so very blessed. And gas chamber training really wasn't so bad after all. It was a piece of cake.

Erin Brophey

Erin Brophey grew up in North Canton, Ohio. She attended the University of Pennsylvania where she earned a Bachelor of Arts in Economics and Political Science degree. She also received her commission in the US Army as a Second Lieutenant upon graduating from Penn.

Erin served as a Medical Service Corps Officer for the US Army for three years active duty and an additional ten years in the US Army Reserves.

She has three children, Will, Luke and Lauren Paschke. She currently lives in Charlotte, North Carolina, and enjoys spending time with her family and dog Patton, swimming, boating, and writing.

Connect with Erin at https://www.instagram.com/erinbrophey.

CHAPTER 6

A Train to Tomorrow: Journey Beyond the Known

Farah Ismail

---

*To my beloved daughters, Hana and Samah. You are
my inspiration, my source of strength, and my greatest
joy. May you always walk with courage, grace, and the
unwavering belief in your limitless potential. I love you to
the moon and back.*

There are moments in life when the journey seems clear, even if the
destination is a mystery. Some might argue it is a good thing. But
having been there, I can tell you the vagueness of the destination felt
anything but 'good'.

I was 46 and a newly single mother of a 6-year-old daughter. I had
made the decision to restart my life. I did not know where it would take

me. But worse, I had no confidence. I only knew I wanted to give my daughter the most loving space to grow and thrive.

Honestly, I was scared, uncertain of what was coming next. You see, no one tells you how to be a single mom 101. Society does not model what to expect when you have to navigate it alone. The going was tough and I was not tough enough to get going. Yet.

The heartbreak, anger and grief weighed heavy. But they could not outweigh the fear I felt in being responsible for another life. I was worried about my daughter's future. I felt like I was flying a plane about to crash. My past experiences were pulling me down.

I had forgotten the bold and brave Farah. I was so full of fear and self-doubt and it paralyzed me. I was reluctant to take risks.

With this fear looming over me, the idea of stepping beyond what was familiar and comfortable filled me with unease and apprehension. I found myself grappling with all the reasons and excuses for my struggles in life, convincing myself it was simply meant to be. I resolved to tackle it all on my own, keeping everything bottled up inside.

I came to realize that I was merely reacting to day-to-day situations, trapped in a cycle of frustration yet refusing any support. I was feeling overwhelmed and powerless to even make small decisions, unable to see clearly ahead in the blur of uncertainty.

Those were the only thoughts I allowed to take root in my mind. I had forgotten how to dream.

The person I once knew had vanished, replaced by someone confined within the walls of her own mind.

Until one day, I reached a breaking point. I grew tired of the resistance, the fear and the self-doubts. I was tired of hiding, feeling unworthy, and being imprisoned by my own thoughts.

This was a profound moment.

Tears were streaming down my face. I knew in some ways I'd made room to dream once more. I began yearning for a life of greater freedom, of being adventurous and carefree, of loving and living freely.

I made a decision.

I decided to slow down and listen to my innermost desires, to reconnect with my soul an envision the life I wanted for both of us. The answer that came back was simple – It doesn't matter which route you take. Just begin with a small step, see what it teaches you, and take a new one from there. I smiled as I felt a sense of ease and lightness.

I planned a weekend trip for my daughter and me to Mysore, a 2-hour train ride from our city. Physically close, yet emotionally distant, it felt like a journey spanning a lifetime of fears, doubts, and uncertainties. Despite being a seemingly ordinary trip, saying YES to simply taking the trip became a symbolic leap of faith for me.

The train ride itself was a remarkable experience. It felt like my first journey ever, exhilarating and filled with love as my daughter and I hugged each other closely.

I got off that train freer than I'd ever been. I felt as though I had found myself, my true self, right there on that train. I felt full to the brim with love for my daughter, my life and my experiences.

Arriving at the resort I had booked, it felt like stepping into heaven. We laughed, played, and bonded deeply, experiencing joy and love in abundance. A sense of calm and excitement washed over me. In that moment, I knew without a doubt that I was exactly where I was meant to be. In touch with being alive.

Those two days were the sweetest and most life-changing of my life. Words cannot capture the profound transformation that occurred. All I know is that it changed me. It helped me break free from my fears and self-imposed limitations, stepping into a new realm of self-belief and possibilities.

That train ride was my ticket to freedom from my inner fears and self-doubt. It felt like a giant leap, shedding the confines of who I thought I was and embracing who I dared to become.

Looking back now, I realize it did not require extraordinary willpower or sacrifice. I chose freedom. I stepped towards freedom with one courageous step forward. I refused to allow fear to be my constant companion. The exhilaration of stepping into a space larger than my fears was indescribable.

This newfound courage propelled me to break free from my limited thinking, to embark on a journey of new beginnings. Breaking out of this mental prison meant traversing from fear to courage, from struggle to hope. I understood then that my past did not dictate my future, unless I chose to dwell there.

Since then, so much has changed.

And there is one change I made on the inside that shifted everything. It came from a way of being Committed. I pledged to be more loyal to my dreams than to my fears.

This marked a turning point, a fresh start.

I began to live in a realm of creation and possibilities. I learnt that things seem impossible because we can't imagine doing them, not because they can't be done.

My daughter fearlessly pursued her dreams and embraced new challenges. Transitioning from a top student in grade 8 to an international school, she ignored doubts about her abilities, dreaming bigger each day. She secured admission to Cambridge University, spending four years expanding her horizons.

Watching her graduate, I reflected on how she dreamt of a different future from her school days and chose to be brave, despite the scary path.

In the years that followed, I, too, fearlessly delved into meaningful work, disrupting my 25-year career in leadership development to expand into coaching. I aspired to be the foremost courage coach globally. I kept learning, growing, and serving.

My coaching practice evolved into a laboratory of courage, aimed at uncovering what truly empowers us to fear less and live our dreams. Inspired by this journey, I built a prosperous, ethical, and sustainable coaching practice. I began coaching leaders, changemakers, and entrepreneurs, unlocking their courage to reimagine their lives, businesses, and careers.

I also noticed that many brilliant clients couldn't see their own brilliance. They didn't realize they were ready to pursue their dreams, do the work they longed for, and bring their visions to reality.

Thus, Courage to Soar was born—my signature coaching program, a portal to freedom and possibility, encouraging individuals to play bigger in their lives and careers. When one is more loyal to their dreams than their fears, the possibilities are endless.

While I would never have scripted my life this way, I am overwhelmed with gratitude for the work I now get to do every day, serving others. It's beyond what I could have envisioned. I'm grateful not only for what I get to do but also for who I have become—and who I am becoming.

Through this journey, I learned that our work in the world is a playground for our soul's growth. Challenges often kick-start that growth. So rather than situations happening TO you, perhaps they are happening FOR you— for your expansion and, dare I say, for your very soul.

Fear will always be along for the ride. And guess what happens when you face fear and do what you must do anyway? You fear less and do it anyway. That's called Courage!

The greatest rewards are reserved for those with the greatest courage. We all get knocked down from time to time. We all encounter challenging circumstances. This will never change.

You have the power to get back up. Always. Never forget.

The unknown can be intimidating, but it's also where the magic happens. Each step forward is a testament to your courage and resilience. The path might not always be clear, but with unwavering faith in your dreams, you will navigate it successfully. Every moment is an opportunity to grow, to learn, and to become the person you were meant to be. The adventure is yours to define, and the possibilities are truly limitless.

Most importantly, understand that whatever you dream of, this moment is a step on the path to get there. Everything you've been through has brought you right here. Everything you've experienced has prepared you for what happens next. What will happen next?

That's the adventure.

Farah Ismail

Farah Ismail is an Internationally recognized Facilitator, Executive Coach, Author and Founder of Interact Consulting.

She draws on 25+ years of practical experience in the fields of leadership and personal development. Working with her is not your typical coaching experience. She wakes you up to your true potential.

Farah has always been highly adventurous. It all started when she was young and she dreamt of doing her MBA in the USA. When she finally got accepted by a reputed University, she couldn't go. She was heartbroken. But then… she did get her MBA. At age 40! A trek – a Masters of Beginners in Adventure – that challenged her limits and allowed her to question what she thought was possible.

Her adventures have taken her far: flying for an airline, working across cultures and exploring the world all expanded her vision. Years later, she had the bold dream of starting her own facilitation and coaching business. She believes that the biggest adventure you can take is to live the life of your dreams.

Some adventures also came in the form of life's lessons.

After going through a few life-changing experiences, Farah felt powerless. She later understood that it's in deciding who she wants to be rather than what she wants to do that she could turn her life around for the better. Her life lessons became the catalyst for her greatest personal growth.

Today, it is her passion to be a courage catalyst for others. She inspires you to stop dreaming and start living your dream.

Connect with Farah at https://www.coachfarah.com/.

CHAPTER 7

Choose Yourself

Greta Kay

---

*I dedicate this chapter to women who are ready to take
risks and make bold decisions to change their lives
and choose themselves over abusive relationships or
addictions.*

When we come into this life, almost instantly we start making decisions. Even as a baby we choose to cry, choose to like or dislike someone. As human beings, we have a power to decide. Every decision, small or big, shapes our lives. When we decide to change, we grow.

My story. My childhood was full of fear, abuse and worry. As a kid, I was always scared and confused. My parents were drinking and fighting all the time. I could not understand why they couldn't just stop.

Unfortunately, later on I understood all too well. I started smoking at age 14, drinking and using drugs at 18, and fell into multiple abusive relationships. I was physically and mentally abused by several men and I kept making the decision to stay. I was literally drinking myself to death and kept making a decision to drink again and again. I wasn't a good mom, but kept making a decision to stay the same. My relationships got worse and worse over years. I was at the very bottom for years and did not have a lot of hope to get out. A few bold decisions saved me and changed my life forever. Now I am healthy, happy, wealthy, confident, respected and loved.

The very first bold decision I made was to leave an abusive relationship when I was 20 years old. I met this powerful man when I was very young, he got me into using drugs and fully controlled my life. He mentally and physically abused me almost every day. I had nowhere to go, I could not support myself, my parents lived abroad, and I felt hopeless. When I was four months pregnant, he choked me. The only reason he let go was because he thought I was dead. I survived and it opened my eyes. It was not about me anymore; I had a child to protect. I decided to run away. I knew if he caught me that would have been the last time. I had no money or extra clothes, but somehow made it to the city where my brother lived and he bought me a ticket to United States. I came to the US not knowing anything, but I knew I was safe. This decision was one of the hardest decisions I made, but it saved our lives.

Ten years later, I decided to go back to Europe and before I knew it, I got back together with that man and found myself fighting for my life once again. I was filled with hope that since we had a daughter everything would change. That wasn't the case. He almost killed me several times in front of my daughter, so I made a decision to leave again.

Another bold and one of the hardest decisions I had to make was beating my additions. I drank and smoked for over 15 years and used drugs for two. Every day I waited to come home from work so I could have a drink. But it was never one drink. It was a bottle … or two. Every day was a fight. I could not stop. I could not sleep, socialize or do anything without alcohol. I would drink and smoke until I passed out. It turned into binge drinking where I drank for weeks without getting up, eating or drinking water. I had to go to the hospital for detox, because I could not sober up by myself. My body got weaker and weaker. My mind was a mess. I made the worst decisions, hung out with the worst people, at the worst places. I lived a double life pretending to be normal during the day just to go home and abuse myself once again. My addictions were holding me hostage in my own body. I spent one year in and out of a detox hospital 14 times, yes 14!

I got pregnant with my second child and had no choice but to stop. I truly thought I was cured. I counted the days till I could drink again. I thought because I did not drink for so long I could now be a social drinker again. It took one month of my social drinking to end up in a hospital again. This time was different. This time I knew I tried everything I knew. That was the day I made a decision to stop drinking forever. I knew deep down within my soul this time was the last time. I haven't had a drink in over eight years and haven't smoked in over four. And I never will.

Once I got stronger and healthier I made another decision to quit my day job and open my own business and built a life I could only dream of. My life changed forever. I enjoy every single minute of it. I am surrounded by wonderful people, love and respect.

I want to share with you the steps to help you get out of any stressful situation. After all, stress is a huge factor that causes people to become addicted.

Decision. When you are trying to leave any situation, the first step is to make a very strong decision. Next step is to keep making that decision every day for the rest of your life. The best decision you can ever make is to choose yourself. Choose YOU over an addiction, abusive relationship or a stressful job. Making a decision to stay in an abusive relationship could cost you your life. Situations and people don't change; only you can change and decide to leave the situation. This life is about you and everyone around you can only help you learn your lessons. Don't feel sorry for another person or try to save someone else. They have their own lessons to learn. You need to save yourself. There is always a way out of any situation. There is always another option that is better for you. You cannot expect anything new if you don't let go of what is old.

Get healthy. When you leave a stressful situation or decide to beat your addictions, it is very important to improve your mental, physical and spiritual health. There are so many things out there; choose what works best for you. When you feel healthy, you feel strong and more confident about your new journey. You can only improve your life if you get out of low frequencies. The way to get into higher frequencies and attract better things in life is to improve your physical and spiritual health, to forgive yourself, to heal your inner child, to make peace with your past, forgive your parents or previous partners, get rid of anger and pain, and everything will start changing. Love yourself for who you are and take care of yourself. Only then you can attract people who will do the same.

Never go back. Whatever you do, do NOT go back, don't even look back. It will never get better; it will only get worse. From my own experience of going back so many times, I can guarantee you that situations don't change. If someone abused you once, they will keep doing that until one time could be the last. If you drink one drink, smoke one cigarette or use drugs just one time, you will end up at your lowest again. It is just a matter of time.

Gratitude. Once you make a decision to change your life, enjoy every minute of it. Watch how everything changes around you and focus on positives. There is no point of making a decision, going through pain and feeling like a victim. A lot of people still hold on to the past, thinking of how it could have been or what if. Some people feel angry, can't let go of the pain. What they don't understand is that it only harms them and can cause a lot of physical pain, or even illness. Some people blame others for their addictions or misery. There is no one to blame! At the end of the day, YOU chose to be with those people in those particular situations. You chose to drink, smoke, or use drugs. You have to look at yourself and ask why, what did it teach me? Learn and move on. Every person is able to make a decision. Someone can make a decision to hurt you, but you can make a decision to leave or let them hurt you again.

Practice gratitude every single day. Be thankful for everything, the things you have and don't have yet. It will help you in your healing journey and it will attract better things and people.

My life was not easy, but it made me who I am today. I am able to help others and am grateful for that. You are in charge of your life. Choose to make the best out of it. Only through pain do we grow. Bold decisions are the decisions that will change your life. Whatever decision you make, make sure you choose yourself first. Only when you are strong, happy, and healthy you can spread the love around you.

You ARE strong enough to leave any situation.

You are strong enough to heal.

You are strong enough to choose YOU!

Greta Kay

Greta Kay is a mother of two beautiful children, author, alcohol addiction coach, leader, businesswoman.

From her traumatic childhood and struggling with multiple addictions and hardships, she was able to transform into a successful, respected and healthy woman who is helping others change their life forever.

She is the author of the book *"Circle of Wine"* and co-author of the book *"The Mind-Body Connection."*

Connect with Greta at https://linktr.ee/gretakay.

CHAPTER 8

Follow Your Instincts and Just Do It

Jacalyn Price

---

*I dedicate this chapter to my DAD; he has just turned
93 years old. He is now in permanent care, we lost Mum
nearly five years ago. Dad has coped very well, he loves
where he is now, we can all visit regularly. He always has a
smile on his face.*

---

*Your intuition is the compass I gifted you so you can
navigate the seas of life; trust that inner voice.*
The Universe

Flying Through the Air With Ease

The first a-bit-scary-at-the-time **risk** was going up in an ultralight plane. There was only the pilot and me. It was a clear, still morning, no breeze. We flew for about 20 minutes over the land and towards the ocean fairly low to the ground. It was quite breathtaking.

Due to the reward of making the decision to go and then enjoying amazing sights, I would do it all over again. Take the risk to make the decision and say yes to the opportunity.

As Sir Richard Branson says,
Say yes and work out how to do it later.

It's Not About the Competition; It's About the Journey

After winning $5,000 in a travel competition, my next **risk**, I was still on a walking frame and crutches when I made the decision to travel to England with a family member. Dad had a half-sister he had never met. A long but rewarding flight to England from Australia, we met Ivy (who was then in her 70s) who lived alone in the town of Smethwick not far from Birmingham. We talked a lot, learning family history.

Ivy had never left her small town; but we spent a week in London. We took Ivy on a river cruise down the Thames and looked at other sites while there. Ivy was so excited. We went to Buckingham Palace and saw the changing of the guards, visited Windsor Castle, travelled on the bullet train to Paris and went up the Eiffle Tower. WOW! The view from the top is spectacular. The rewards of travelling to England, being able to see Ivy, visiting the town of York where my grandmother (Dad's mum) came from. Being in a country I'd never been before, learning more of the family history in England was so rewarding.

With the remaining travel money, we went to New Zealand. Even though I live in Australia and am close, that was my first time there.

My grandparents lived in New Zealand in the 1920s and had a truck and lorry business in Wellington. We visited the house, the school, the business location, and the wall my grandfather built to protect the business in case of earthquakes. We visited lots of places, travelled on the cable car in Wellington. Again, the view from the top was absolutely amazing. We had family there, near Christchurch, a cousin and we were able to visit her as well. We hadn't seen her in many years. Janette took us to other places to see the sights, always making the most of the opportunity that comes along. It's so rewarding.

I'm a Firewalker

My next big **risk** was while attending the Unleash the Power Within event with Tony Robbins. He does a Firewalk ceremony where attendees walk across a bed of over 1000 degrees of hot coals. I decided to do the Firewalk and learned that it's all in your mindset, the power of the subconscious mind, imagining we're walking over cool moss instead of those coals. You can feel the heat from the pits before you walk. I (along with hundreds of others) did the Firewalk. I said, "If I can Firewalk, I can do anything."

About five years later, I did the Firewalk for the second time. I was one of the crew this time (which I highly recommend for anyone getting into the personal development space that wants to grow) assisting attendees at the event and even during the Firewalk making sure as they were walking, they were okay.

Being Asked and Saying "Yes"

While attending a networking course with speaker Matt Morris, next **risk**, I was asked if I would like to co-author a book with him. Of course

I said "Yes." I have always wanted to write a book and the opportunity had not presented itself before. *Breakthrough Leadership* with Jacalyn Price, along with 29 leading experts including Matt Morris, would become my first book of many.

The synchronicity of that book led me to joining an author's group, which led to my next **risk**, co-authoring now with Lynda Sunshine West and Sally Larkin Green and other authors. Having a book gives you authority and credibility and leads to more opportunities.

I am now co-authoring with Debbie Small, the eZWay family, Sunil Tulsiani, and Brian Tracy. I have an article in the "WOW" Women of Worth Magazine and the Bx xClusive Magazine. Always being open-minded and ready to say yes to the opportunities that come my way has led me to places I never imagined.

The books have led to more opportunities, podcast interviews with Sara Troy, Sherri Leopold, Dr. Scott Fox, Faye Waterman, Misty Henkel, and more, as well as speaking opportunities.

Trust Your Instinct

Your confidence grows more with each new opportunity that presents itself. Always obey your instinct because it will never let you down.

While attending an author's networking event with Lynda Sunshine West and Sally Larkin Green, there was an opportunity to win two prizes: 1) attend Prosperity Camp (a $7,500 USD ticket) or 2) attend Secret Knock (a $5,000 USD ticket). Just for fun, I said to Lynda, "What are the dates? I'll book my flights."

At the end of the networking event, Lynda announced that I won, and I could choose the event I wanted to attend. I chose Prosperity Camp.

It was a trip to San Diego, California, from Australia (more than 7,000 miles) to attend. I said if this Prosperity Camp is worth 7k, I'm going.

Next **risk,** I made flight and accommodation arrangements, and attended in January 2024.

The event was run by Greg Reid and other leaders. I was able to meet Lynda Sunshine West in person. It was an amazing two-day event. I met a lot of inspiring leaders, had time in the opportunity chair to share my business and have feedback from everyone.

I spent two weeks in San Diego and met Paulette Ensign, another woman I had taken a course with, and we were able to meet for lunch and catch up about each other's businesses and anything in general.

I also did a lot of sightseeing while there. I visited the Maritime Museum, toured the ship the USS Midway and other ships, enjoyed a sunset cruise, and visited many museums and notable sights including Balboa Park, San Diego Zoo, Cabrillo National Monument and Lookout (what a spectacular view).

I made the most of my time there, visited La Jolla and went into a cave, saw hundreds of birds and sea life, went to the Sunset Cliffs and experienced an amazing sunset over the water. It was breathtaking. I also visited Coronado Island and stayed at an Airbnb close to everything.

I did all of this on my own. You have a gut feeling while travelling, when and where you feel safe to go to.

I took my Enagic K8 water processor so I could have clean, healthy drinking water wherever I travelled and stayed. It's portable, so I took it on my carryon luggage inside the plane.

Opportunities Abound

Opportunities arise regularly, like my new business as an Enagic water distributor. I'm your go-to Hydration Specialist and people call me Water Woman.

This business came about when I was assisting a customer with his NBN and mobile services. I had bronchitis at the time and couldn't seem to shift it. After a few questions, Mark said, "I have a solution for you and it's water." I didn't hesitate to order my Enagic K8 water processor for the life-changing water and I haven't looked back. Your health is your wealth, and your wealth is your health. I took the **risk** to order my Enagic K8 water processor and it has paid off, improving my health.

In June of 2024, I'll be travelling to Okinawa, Japan, for Enagic's 50th anniversary and I'll be joining over 5,000 people to celebrate.

I've taken the risks of flying in an ultralight, travelling to England, New Zealand, San Diego, Japan, Firewalking, being in multi co-authored books, and starting a new business. You never know when an opportunity will present itself and I love saying YES to new opportunities.

Say YES! Once you say YES, the rest will take care of itself.

I wouldn't change anything and look forward to many more opportunities.

If I can do it, so can you.

I'm Jacalyn Price, bestselling author, traveller, business owner, entrepreneur, business coach, mentor.

Hear me Roar; Watch me Soar.

Jacalyn Price

Jacalyn Price won business of the year in Business Services for ACN in 2020, 2021.

She has published articles in the Bx xClusive Magazine, W.O.W. Woman of Worth Magazine, and Newcastle Weekly.

Jacalyn belongs to the following networking groups, Edward Zia, Business at Breakfast, EzWay Family, BconnectedWorld, More Marketing Ideas, Happy Neighborhood Project, Lake Macquarie Women in Business. She has been a host and speaker at networking events.

Jacalyn was a finalist in Hunter Region Business Excellence Awards, Australian Small Business Champions Awards, Australian Women's Small Business Champions Awards, Local Business Awards, Australian Ladies in Business Initiative Awards, Bx Business xCellence Awards.

Jacalyn's key to success is her personal development. Some of her biggest influences include Bob Proctor, Zig Ziglar, Mary Morrisey, Tony Robbins, Peter Sage, Jim Rohn, Grant Cardone, John Maxwell, Simon Sinek to name a few.

After her sister Jen was diagnosed with breast cancer and had to pay a lot for treatments, Jacalyn began her mission of setting up a future foundation for people with illness to access funding for treatments and medications. Jacalyn loves touching hearts and changing lives.

Every day for her is a new day, new strengths, new thoughts and possibilities.

Connect with Jacalyn at www.jacalynp.acnibo.com.

CHAPTER 9

Freedom IS Your Business!

Jennifer M. Clarke

I dedicate this chapter to my children to be blessed beyond measure, to have freedom: time freedom, financial freedom, and location freedom.

Freedom is in my very being. My grandparents built a legacy of freedom that I greatly value and would like to build upon the foundation that they were part of creating for our family. Freedom is vitally important to enjoying life to its fullest capacity.

After having several dreams about owning a sailboat and sailing to specific islands, I took a bold risk. My dream was that we would experience freedom by having a sailboat. I also had dreams about the locations, specific island destinations that would be exciting to explore with our sailboat. I then looked up the locations that were in my dreams and after sailing to them they are now our favorite locations.

My business has provided the opportunity to buy, maintain, and moor a sailboat and the time freedom to sail it. There's an opportunity that comes with building a business that allows you to experience this type of freedom.

To listen to and follow my dreams has been a risk because they have led me to the unknown. The risks are exciting, especially when the literal dream is something that leads to amazingly good experiences. The fresh air, sunshine, salty sea water, and the feeling of relaxation are all so freeing and healing. Having an online business allows me to work from anywhere, including our sailboat. I can see a client or potential client online and then bask in the sun on the deck or swim off the side of the sailboat between appointments.

I would love to see my family and those that I serve in my coaching business become prosperous, successful, healthy, and full of life to be able to enjoy a high level of financial freedom and time freedom. Seeing the gifts and talents that many people have and being part of coaching them to release them through building a business is what I feel called to do. This process can bring healing, prosperity, abundance, and healthy relationships. When we have financial abundance, we have more freedom to pursue the most impactful areas of life, such as spending an abundance of quality time with those we love and contributing in a significant way to their lives and many others.

For many years, I had only pursued service without any thought of financial gain, as I thought that it was better to give and never or hardly ever receive. I volunteered thousands of hours with our church, with children's ministry, directing free children's camps, women's ministry, marriage ministry, retreats, live events, etc. I had to learn, though, that in order to give, we must receive and the more we give, the more we need to receive. One way to receive, while serving and giving to others at the same time, is through building a business.

I've been able to coach my clients to quickly launch, grow, build, and scale their businesses and see how their lives have changed for the better in a short time. I feel joy when I see them traveling all over the world, enjoying tropical beaches, and luxury cruises. When they have the finances and the time freedom to relax and take care of themselves, they can serve their clients at a higher level. They can then give out of the overflow of additional energy, rather than giving out of the resources that they have for their own life and healing. Getting out of survival mode and "fight or flight" allows even more enjoyable experiences to be received in many areas of life.

Encouraging my family and others to live life to the fullest, to pursue perfect health, to obtain their goals, dreams and visions is very important to me. I have a calling to increase the economy of neighborhoods, communities, cities, regions, and nations. Economic development and growth bring location freedom, time freedom, and freedom in general. Embracing freedom in all areas of life brings a full and abundant life, which makes it more enjoyable. Having as many positive experiences as possible is important. They bring healing and create meaningful memories. When people are out of survival mode and feel as though all of their needs and many of their wants are provided for, they can let go of a lot of stress. This process is supportive in eliminating the "fight, flight, or freeze" response to begin truly living life in a way that is genuine, authentic, and relaxing.

Every time that I've taken risks by taking action on my dreams or the subtle promptings of something that I sense that would be good to do, I have had wonderful experiences. Listening and actually implementing my dreams and the small voice has been the most difficult to do. However, when I move forward with following a dream, then I receive a powerful blessing and positive experiences. Every time I don't listen and act on my dreams, visions, or words, I regret it and see how it would have been very beneficial had I taken action on them. Sometimes the consequences have been riskier and have made things harder for me in the long run. I have free will and freedom of choice in many areas of life, similar to the majority of people in this world; however, when I don't follow my dreams or the subtle promptings of what I should do, then I feel like I've missed out on something that could have been so powerful. I miss out on the amazing blessing that would have happened if I had taken the risk to act on my dreams, visions, and goals, which I believe is riskier than not following my dreams and the still, small voice.

I have many regrets of not taking the risk to follow those promptings and leadings because in hindsight the outcome would potentially have been much better. Oftentimes, I try to think about these promptings from a logical, realistic perspective based on what I already know, rather than taking the risk to step out in faith and just take action on what I sense is the direction to move toward. Recently, I decided to just take action when I sensed that I should do something that didn't make sense, logically, and I had a profound healing experience. That experience made me realize how many powerful experiences I have missed out on and how I want to try to keep the momentum moving forward to just follow my dreams, visions, and promptings, even when it doesn't make sense at the time.

Many people have lived in a way that restricts their choices in life, especially when working at a regular job building another company's business. Working for another company can be restrictive when it comes to booking time off and having control over your own schedule. The lack of time freedom is a great reason to create your plan of incorporating time freedom into your life so you can turn your dreams into your reality.

Like many people, you might dream of traveling while running your business from anywhere in the world. Your dreams could include building retreat centers on farms, ranches, or in remote or exotic locations. You may envision building a legacy for your family and establishing non-profit foundations and charitable organizations from the overflow of your business income. Having time freedom will allow you to expand your dreams, visions, and goals to become reality.

Many dreams, visions, and goals have become a reality because of building successful businesses. Taking the risk to build a business and acting on your dreams, visions, and goals is not as risky as not following them. There is a reason for these aspirations, and an exciting experience awaits. Past traumatic experiences, hurt feelings, lack of trust, and other negative situations can hold you back from taking the bold risks that you are meant to take to maximize your positive life experiences.

When I hear my clients' goals, dreams, and visions that are bigger than I have ever dreamt, it encourages me to think and dream bigger. I am committed to doing whatever I can to support all of my clients in accomplishing their amazing goals and visions, leaving a great legacy on this earth, along with FREEDOM, which is all of our Business.

Jennifer M. Clarke

Jen M. Clarke has been a highly successful Business Coach to clients from all over the world. She is known for her expertise in helping Entrepreneurs and Business Owners enroll High Ticket, Premium clients within a day to a few weeks, on average! Jen M. Clarke has many years of experience in building 6 and 7 figure businesses in various fields including financial planning, health & wellness, and retreats. She has also worked for not-for-profit charities and has organized events, retreats, and conferences. She has established herself as a leading authority as a Business Coach.

Jen M. Clarke specializes in helping her clients attract and enroll high ticket, premium clients. She has developed a proven method, called QuickStart Business Method™, and a step-by-step formula that coaches entrepreneurs to position themselves as the authority and experts in their niche & field of expertise. Jen coaches her clients to communicate in a way that is highly effective to build their businesses very quickly when her intellectual proprietary marketing ideas for her clients' businesses are implemented. Jen is known for her customized, engaging, and empowering Business Coaching. She is a speaker and has delivered keynote speeches at live events, retreats, workshops, seminars, conferences, and many other types of events, both in-person and online. Jen has a commitment to excellence in helping her clients succeed so they can reach their full potential! Jen M. Clarke's ultimate vision is for her and her clients to have a significant impact in this world to create a powerful legacy!

Connect with Jen at https://coachjenclarke.com.

CHAPTER 10

Risk, Reward, Repeat

Julie Steelman

To my father who always nurtured me to be my own woman
and lead from my heart.

In the realm of business (and life), the prevailing wisdom often champions the safety of familiarity, the comfort of the known, and the avoidance of risk at any cost. The truth is, we try way too hard to control everything.

Yet, for those of us who defy convention and embrace uncharted territory, the rewards can be monumental. It's how I rapidly generated over $100 million in sales and earned my way out of corporate America at 47 to become an entrepreneur.

Let me take you through a pivotal moment in my career—a moment that underscores the profound impact of inner strength, intuition, and the audacity to take bold risks that pay off.

It all started with what seemed like a catastrophic misstep—an online advertising campaign gone awry, courtesy of an epic blunder involving none other than Apple, my client, led by the iconic Steve Jobs. The epic mistake was discovered by him at a convention minutes after he walked off stage having announced the Intel partnership.

Since I was new to this job, they decided to test me and threw the Apple account over to me. I wasn't even working there when this big blunder happened. How the heck do I fix this?

To add to the complexity of the situation, the advertising agency Apple was using also was home to many other brands we needed to work with. So not only did Apple know, so did all their other clients like Nissan, The CW channel, Sony Playstation, and the list goes on.

Clearly, I was confronted with a formidable challenge: how to not only salvage our relationship with Apple, but also restore our reputation in the industry. It was a pivotal moment that demanded not just strategic thinking but a fundamental shift in perspective.

Taking a deep breath, I embraced the uncertainty that lay ahead with open arms, knowing that it held the potential to reshape our trajectory in unforeseen ways. It was a journey fraught with challenges and obstacles, yet I remained undeterred, driven by a sense of purpose that burned bright within me.

To contemplate this hugely embarrassing mistake, I did what anyone would do; I went to the beach and watched the waves crashing against the shore and listened. I just sat there and listened. I had a revelation: true strength emanates not from control or manipulation, but from vulnerability and authenticity. And making things right meant I had to repair the broken trust, or we were not going to get anywhere.

It was then that I made a decision that defied conventional wisdom—I opted to lead with authenticity, humility, and an unshakable belief in my own capabilities. If there was any chance at salvaging this relationship and my job, I needed to make things right. I knew I had to lead this meeting and do it my way and convince the executive team to let me.

Despite encountering skepticism and resistance from my own CEO and VPs, I remained steadfast in my conviction that I possessed the ability to transform this setback into an opportunity. But it was going to take courage and humility to get anywhere with this very unforgiving client. I knew they would go in there and try to win an argument versus try to find a way forward. I couldn't let that happen.

This decision was not made lightly; it was a rebellious act against the prevailing norms that dictated a more conservative approach. Despite the skepticism and resistance that echoed within top management, I remained resolute in my conviction that within every setback lies the seed of opportunity. Armed with nothing but my intuition and a resolute sense of purpose, I made it my mission to re-establish trust with my clients.

I used my intuition as my compass and stepped into the fray with determination and grit. The first thing I needed to do was meet with the chief technology officer to find out what happened and what we needed to do to fix it. The morning following that meeting, he wrote new computer code that fixed the problem.

My next step was guided by my commitment to lead by example, demonstrating that true leadership transcends the boundaries of fear and doubt and not always trying to please your boss. I called my client and booked the meeting; grateful he said yes to even seeing us after embarrassing ourselves. Luckily, I had long-standing relationships with these people and so they agreed to meet knowing I would never waste their time.

With my heart racing and determination coursing through my veins, I entered that pivotal meeting with Apple, the executive team in tow, intent on not only extending our apologies but also presenting a solution that would surpass their expectations.

Shock coursed through my veins. Not only was the Apple team there, but all the heads of the other brands they represent were there, too. Gulp! Prior to entering the room, I had an argument with the management team in the parking lot, once again convincing them to let me lead the meeting. I even offered to let them fire me if I failed. They happily agreed.

The thing is, I just knew if this east coast crew tried to strong arm a west coast crew instead of focusing on repairing the relationship, telling the truth about what happened and demonstrating how it would never be a problem again, we had no chance of reconciling.

What ensued was nothing short of miraculous. Through a blend of genuine remorse, strategic foresight, and a profound understanding of my client's needs, I not only salvaged our relationship with Apple, but also secured an exclusive multi-million-dollar advertising agreement that would propel one of their flagship products—a deal that would forever alter the trajectory of my career.

In that moment of triumph, I grasped a profound truth: no external force truly dictates our fate—not our employers, not our circumstances, not even our mistakes. We are the architects of our own destinies, guided by an inner wisdom that transcends limitations. And when we dare to place our trust in that wisdom, when we summon the courage to undertake risks that others might shrink from, the rewards can be nothing short of extraordinary.

And guess what? When we take that leap of faith and trust in our gut, the universe responds with a big ol' high-five of epic rewards. Suddenly, doors that were locked tighter than a jar of pickles are swinging wide open, inviting us into a world of endless opportunity. It's like hitting the jackpot, but instead of coins, we're showered with opportunities to grow, shine, and put a real ding on the Universe (see what I did there?).

So here's the deal: let's not get bogged down by the "shoulds" and "can'ts." Instead, let's grab life by the horns, throw caution to the wind, and chase those dreams like they're the last ice cream cone on a hot summer day. With courage as our trusty sidekick and our gut feeling as our compass, let's venture forth into the great unknown, ready to write our own epic adventure. Because when we do, there's no limit to how high we can soar, both in life and in business.

True obstacles aren't setbacks; they are opportunities to evolve, to find that creative spark inside and get busy making things happen. What you think is bold or risky is actually innovation trying to get you to try a new approach.

To all the fearless pioneers and emerging entrepreneurs out there, I've got a message that's going to light a fire under you like never before: it's time to embrace the unknown, listen closely to the whispers of your intuition, and tap into the deep reserves of inner strength that lie within you.

Now, I get it—taking risks can be scary. It's like stepping out onto a tightrope with no safety net below. But here's the thing: when we lean into that fear, when we dare to push past our comfort zones and venture into uncharted territory, that's when the real adventure begins. So, don't let fear hold you back, let risk taking pull you forward.

But let's talk strategy for a minute, because let's face it, a little strategic planning never hurts anyone. When it comes to taking those big, bold leaps, it pays to have a game plan. Take the time to assess the risks, weigh your options, and make informed decisions that align with your goals and values. And remember, it's not about playing it safe—it's about being smart and strategic in your approach, ensuring that every move you make brings you one step closer to your dreams.

Above all else, trust yourself. Believe in your abilities, your instincts, and your vision for the future. Because when you trust yourself, when you embrace the uncertainty with open arms, the universe has a funny way of conspiring in your favor.

Julie Steelman

Meet Julie Steelman, a celebrated feminine business mentor dedicated to empowering female entrepreneurs (especially those over 50) with powerful income growth strategies. Julie's journey is marked by extraordinary achievements, including a life-altering money mindset breakthrough in her corporate career which enabled her to rapidly generate $100 million in sales and achieve financial freedom at the young age of 47. Now, Julie is on a mission to empower women to turn their passionate gifts into thriving businesses.

With a master's degree in spiritual psychology and certification as a Woman-Centered coach, Julie offers a proven formula for women to turn their soul work into life-long income. Her transition from corporate success to entrepreneurial mentorship uniquely positions her to understand the challenges and opportunities faced by women in business.

For over four decades, Julie has been trusted and loved by women worldwide. Her proven step-by-step system is meticulously crafted for feminine entrepreneurs who aspire to consistently increase their income, establish real businesses, and live richly abundant lives.

Whether you're seeking to break free from money blocks, accelerate your income, or build a thriving business, Julie is here to lead the way. Join the countless women who have increased their earning potential under Julie's mentorship and build a real business that gives you a richly abundant life.

Connect with Julie at https://juliesteelman.com.

CHAPTER 11

Journey Through Risk

Marilen Jordas Crump

Dedicated to my best friend and husband, Kenny.

How would you define risk, and in what area of life are you prepared to accept it?

I want to emphasize that my children's safety is something I would never risk lightly. I would never willingly engage in activities that pose a significant danger to life or home. Having stated that, I believe we can choose to experience the world in various ways. Risk, reward, experiences, and lessons often intermingle and exchange roles, depending on the journey we undertake.

My personal path has been centered on being an entrepreneur since my senior year of college. I had observed my parents' lifestyle, which was a never-ending cycle of constant work. Their faces were always worn down by clocking in hours of work every week. We took infrequent vacations, and they would constantly argue about money. And it wasn't just them... the world seemed to be filled with unhappy working people who just seemed to be getting by begrudgingly in careers they didn't enjoy. In my mind, I decided that I needed to experience life differently. I would not have a "boss" or a "job."

I began engaging in activities that brought me joy, and almost immediately, I was offered work as a freelance actress and model, dance instructor, web designer, and professional film photographer. It was incredible, and I was able to start my adult life on my own terms. However, this did not make my parents proud or happy. They were highly disappointed in my choices, and they made their feelings known in no uncertain terms. I was saddened by their point of view, and it hurt me to receive such strong discouragement from the people I loved. I nevertheless was determined to stay the course.

Did this mean that I was an instant success? Of course not. But this early choice shaped my perspective on what it means to be an entrepreneur. It was a cocktail of loneliness, excitement, fear, anxiety, creativity, and self-trust. I learned quickly that accepting failure at times was a great trade-off from the restraint of having to show up in a mundane career and being in the same place at the same time, day after day... after day... after... day....

For several years this lifestyle suited me very well. I didn't have insurance or a retirement plan - which to most people seemed reckless and foolish. I actually didn't think about that much as I was involved in other creative processes. I was living for the moment, and I would run into friends who were settled in high-paying careers with all the benefits. Seeing the pride in their faces would sometimes make me question whether I should follow their example and quit my freelance lifestyle.

One day, as I was preparing for a modeling gig in Washington D.C., I stopped by to see my good friends. Upon entering their apartment, I found them staring blankly at the television, speechless and in shock. I wondered what they had been watching. It turned out they were employed by WorldCom, which had been involved in a major scandal. Instantly, their jobs and 401ks vanished. Their world was turned upside down, and all that good feeling of wealth and stability was gone. I saw the effect it had on their self-worth, and in a weird opposite turn, I felt fortunate that I didn't equate my value to a job that could be obliterated at any instant because of a corporate failure.

Undoubtedly, the pandemic has had a similar impact on millions of people worldwide. A recent study highlighted that the cumulative job loss in 2020 reached 23 million. This underscores the widespread suffering many have endured through no fault of their own. Interestingly, my business grew during the pandemic. I share this not to brag, but to inspire you to make bold decisions that may differ from the norm and discover that such out-of-the-box thinking could lead to rewarding outcomes.

I am fortunate to share a similar outlook on life with my husband, Kenny, who held a management position at Verizon for many years. Despite his stable job, the constant layoffs made it feel like a game of musical chairs, with the ever-present threat of his position being eliminated in a downsizing reduction in force, also known as a RIF. We decided together that he should take early retirement, a decision we made right after purchasing our dream home in 2019.

This move was certainly risky. Not only were my parents deeply nervous, but my in-laws were also terrified about our prospects. They questioned how we would maintain our larger property on a single income. Moreover, they wondered how our family could survive on my entrepreneurial earnings alone.

Less than a year later, when the pandemic hit, we felt that the timing was a blessing and our decision was timely indeed. We found ourselves residing on a beautiful waterfront property with a spacious yard for our children to enjoy. Our home was truly ideal for social distancing and both sets of grandparents were able to spend time with us as a pod without any fear that we were exposing ourselves to other people. After all, we were both already by choice working from home.

Sometimes you don't know that when you choose an uncertain path, it will eventually be revealed that it was the setup needed for eventual success. Perhaps I can be bold in many ways because I have a strong faith life that keeps me in sync with the universe and how much love it holds for me. I truly believe that when I am aligned with God, it gives me the tools to lean on intuition for my choices rather than relying on the opinions of others that may themselves be misguided.

I seldom perceive risk in my decisions because they are grounded in experience, research, innovation, love, service, and faith. As I have experienced so many wonderful outcomes with this combination, it has been my mission to help others. I do this as an advocate for helping develop mindsets and businesses. I encourage people to pursue their most creative paths so that they can express their passion and discover ways to monetize it.

Let my contributions here and elsewhere remind you that there are more opportunities than setbacks. Furthermore, there's no true loss if you learn from every situation and are willing to change your approach when necessary.

I continually strive to stay ahead of the curve by participating in insightful discussions about future possibilities. I see that the world is about to be rocked again by a different wave that is AI-driven. I feel that in this day and age the biggest risk you take is ignorance and putting your head in the sand when it comes to technological and cultural advances. How can you be the one in your circle to think differently in order to be prepared for any outcome?

If you are seeking advice from someone like me when it comes to developing yourself in ways that could be an advantage for the future, here it is:

- Give yourself the freedom to reinvent yourself as many times as you like.

- Be around people who push you to advance yourself in knowledge and encourage your happiness.

- Practice goodwill towards yourself and encourage others to do the same. When we are internally happy with who we are, we can reflect that in how we care for others.

- Assess your IKIGAI (Purpose) regularly by asking
  - What do I love?
  - What am I good at?
  - What can I get paid for?
  - What does the world need?

- Learn about my D.R.E.A.M. Success Strategy™, which stands for DIRECTION, RELIQUISH, EFFICIENCY, ACTION, MOMENTUM >> Accomplish your goals using these 5 powerful and proven steps!

- Do your research… Read books, listen to podcasts, attend workshops and trainings, get involved within communities that you want to succeed in, and collect knowledge from everywhere you can.

As for me, my next steps are learning about ways to quadruple my earnings by starting innovative ventures like my new brands called IntuSuccess™ and MTEAMAI™, which I am simultaneously launching to help serve more entrepreneurs. If that includes you, then I hope you will continue to stay connected with me beyond reading this chapter. I hope to have demonstrated enough personal evidence of success, even in the face of disbelief from others or challenging circumstances. Remember, you have the choice to persist and persevere beyond perceived risks.

Marilen Jordas Crump

Marilen Crump, the visionary CEO and Founder of ArtInspired, LLC, is a force to be reckoned with in the business world. As the head of a diverse portfolio of brands, including IntuSuccess™, $1k in a Day Program™, and MTEAMAI™, she empowers her clients to turn their dreams into reality by helping them create successful new businesses.

Marilen's passion for making a difference extends beyond the business realm. She generously lends her expertise and time as a board member of the Youth Volunteer Corps of Hampton Roads, where she actively contributes to the development of young minds and the betterment of the community. Additionally, her commitment to fostering economic growth is evident in her position on the board of the York County Chamber of Commerce.

A graduate of Sweet Briar College in Virginia, Marilen's education paved the way for her career as a Business Developer and Marketing Strategist. Her keen insight and strategic acumen have made her a sought-after professional in her field.

Beyond her professional achievements, Marilen's talents extend into the world of arts and entertainment. An accomplished Ballroom Dancer, Actress, and Singer, she brings grace, passion, and creativity to every stage she graces.

Marilen's success as a leader, professional, and artist is further enriched by her role as a devoted mother of five children. Supported by her loving husband, Kenneth, she skillfully balances the demands of her professional and personal life, proving that dedication and determination can lead to remarkable achievements.

Connect with Marilen at https://marilencrump.com.

CHAPTER 12

When I Listened

Mary Elizabeth Jackson

---

*I dedicate this chapter to all of the women and men in
hopes that they will listen to their inner guidance and
nudgings to live a more empowered life.
Anything is possible.*

L ife is filled with risks each day. We certainly experience this from
the time we take our first breath. We don't know as we grow if we
will succeed in that next step without some sort of failure or challenge.
Moving forward and trying is part of our core. Avoiding risks means
missing out on valuable life lessons and blessings. Like you, I have
taken risks and failed and taken chances and experienced some wonders
in my life.

A literal two years passed, during which I felt a persistent nudge or poke on my right shoulder. Did I listen? Not until I stopped and paid attention did my life change. Not only for me, but for my entire family. In 2013, I had a very late in life surprise baby. My son's birth and my recovery were very challenging, and we didn't know if we would both survive. In the aftermath of my recovery, sitting in a deep space of gratitude for my life and my sons, came a precious story. In those few moments, precious words were divinely downloaded and would become a significant part of my life and journey.

I ignored the urging for two years due to self-doubt about my writing ability. I thought, *I am just a mom, and I should just save this for my children one day when they are older.* With the push from the other side not giving up, I finally stopped and listened. One day I said out loud, "Ok what? What is it that you want me to do? I have no idea where or how to start or whom to talk to."

Curious and clueless about publishing, I sought advice from an academically published friend. The joke was on me because book genres are like islands. Nowadays, there are many publishing houses, presses, and boutiques that cater to different genres. However, at that time, there was no one I asked who knew about children's books or publishing for kids. The doors opened after this man I asked said to me, "I want to introduce you to someone, and I think you two will hit it off." I had no idea that the man he introduced me to would be the next step in my journey.

Thornton Cline and I met in 2015, and he already had eight books published. When we finally got together, he read everything I had been writing since my son was born. After the experience I had while nursing my son, poetry and words just started flowing out and I began keeping a notebook with me. Inspiration could strike anytime, and I didn't want to miss it. I still do this today and also make use of my phone's voice recorder.

Among all my writings from those two years, Thornton selected the story I wrote while nursing my son. The story, divinely downloaded during intense gratitude two years prior, the one God kept tapping my shoulder and saying, "You need to do something with this story."

Thornton then asked me, "Can I write ten songs to go with this book?" I had just met him and had no knowledge of his achievements as a "Dove award nominee" or his prolific songwriting career. He wrote "Love is the Reason," that Gloria Gaynor and Englebert Humperdinck famously recorded. But I responded "Yes" before I realized the words slipped out. *Who am I to decline such an offer? This is so cool*, I thought to myself.

In the next week, Thornton came to my house with ten sweet precious lullabies he wrote and played on my keyboard. Occupational Therapy was working with my little son in the other room as I sat and cried listening to Thornton as he played them for me. The songs were a perfect match for my feelings about the story, its meaning, and my intention to share it with others. The next thing I knew, my daughters were in his studio recording the songs which set in motion their music career together.

An illustrator was next on the agenda, and I casually asked the art teacher at my daughters' school if she would experiment with some drawings. Again, perfection for this little story. Everything was coming together. Things fell into place, one after another. It was like magic. Exploring new paths opened countless doors.

Then the last walk up the mountain of risk and bold challenges was finding a publisher. Thornton was already published, so he knew how to pitch. We wrote what we believed was a powerful marketing plan to go along with the pitch. It took us a few months of sending out many pitches and queries, but we finally found a traditional publisher in Texas. It was unbelievable that all of this was happening.

Perfectly Precious Poohlcious (that was its first name, Now *Perfectly Me* by a new publisher) was published February 9, 2017. It's like the birth of your child; you never forget the date. The title came when I looked at my little baby. So sweet and innocent, facing numerous challenges and those are the words I heard. The premise is that we love our babies, regardless of how they come into life. We see their perfection no matter what and it's important for us to teach them to accept themselves and others just as we all are.

Three months after the book launched, it won a Gold Maxy Literary Award. I was amazed and disbelieving at all that occurred in this small story born from love and gratitude. The impact of words from a single moment can be profound for us and others. Since then, two other books have been written to accompany the first and all three books have received four- and five-star Readers' Favorites. The first book was relaunched as The Inspired Kid Series, reaching #1 in new releases on Amazon and first readers for children.

Taking that chance on myself has led to numerous opportunities, most of which I couldn't have foreseen years ago. In 2017, God directed me to produce a show for authors. I was unsure of what I was doing or how to proceed. Again, I heard the words DO IT ANYWAY. My friend and I wanted to start live streaming back then and the online platform was growing. We started the Writers Corner Live show, which we have been doing author interviews for six years now, and the show is about to go onto Roku, Amazon Fire, and Google TV. We have met and interviewed people from around the globe, from debut to indie, to multi award winners to New York Times Best Sellers.

Another door opened in 2022 when I was getting some music reviews for my daughters-Sisters J written up. The owner of the PR company said, "I like what you do, and I want an author podcast for my PR company. Will you do it?" It took me six months to say yes. I was uncertain about the podcast success or additional commitments. Taking that risk and being bold enough to believe I could landed me this past January 2024 to join the Brushwood Media Network and syndicated radio. At the present time, Cover to Cover has over 340,000 listeners worldwide. Absolutely an unexpected event. Every time I have prayed to God asking about quitting or continuing always yields the same answer—YES, keep going, don't give up. You will meet some of the most amazing and influential people and this is exactly what has happened.

I've met some of the most incredible, successful, and famous people I could ever dream of. And it all goes back to taking a bold risk on myself. Among those people, Lynda Sunshine West and Sally Larkin Green stand out as great champions for all of us. This will be my fifth anthology with Action Takers Publishing and there is a local coffee shop that sells these books every week. This happened because I said yes to sharing my stories with others. Sharing my journey in the anthologies encouraged me to talk about events I never had publicly and in doing that I stepped more into the truth of me and who I am.

I have not made a million dollars, not even hundreds of thousands of dollars. I haven't conquered corporations or risen to the top of a multibillion-dollar company. Not found the cure for cancer or how to get all of us off social media more. But my bold risk has given me huge rewards in my life. I am grateful for every step. Taking those bold risks in your life is worth it! Experiences beyond your wildest dreams can happen, but you will never know if you never try.

Mary Elizabeth Jackson

Mary Elizabeth Jackson is a five-time #1 Amazon Bestselling author in the collaborative anthology *Glimpses into the World of Autism,* and #1 International Bestsellers *Women with Healing Gifts; The Fearless Entrepreneurs; Invisible No More, Invincible Forever More* (Aug 2021); and *The Book I Read* (March 2022).

Jackson is also the 2017 Gold Maxy award-winning author of the children's book *Perfectly Precious Poohlicious.* Jackson just released her Inspired Kids series with book one *Perfectly Me* (Norns Triad Publications 2023) #1 in new releases for beginner reader's book, Book 2 *Look at Me*, and Book 3 *The Wonder of Me* (Norns Triad Publications). Jackson focuses on writing empowering books for kids and adults.

Jackson is also a ghostwriter, collaborator, educator, speaker, hit songwriter, the voice for the Sports2Gether app, and manager of singing duo Sisters J.

Mrs. Jackson is a certified special needs advocate and an Ambassador Advocate for AutismTn. Jackson is also an advocate advisor for the Global non-profit Billion-Strong. She co-founded and co-hosts Writers

Corner Live TV, and Special Needs TV Shows that air on Amazon Live, Facebook, Twitter, LinkedIn, and YouTube. Jackson is a radio talk show host of Cover to Cover on the Brushwood Media Network. She is also a contributing writer for WOW WARRIOR online Magazine.

Mrs. Jackson is a very busy mom, wife, empath, and intuitive. She loves nature, being creative, anything funny, and inspiring others to believe in themselves to go from where they are to their full potential. She lives with her hubby, three kids, and a dog in the Nashville area.

~Cherish every moment of life.

Connect with Mary at www.maryejackson.com.

CHAPTER 13

My Beginning

Mary-Frances Buckland

The words of my daughter were full of fear and courage as she pushed her way between her father and me. "Dad, just stop! Can't you see that she doesn't love you anymore? Just let her go!" These are words that no 16-year-old should have to say pleading for her mother's life.

My husband had come into the living room with a look in his eyes I had never seen before. He was holding a gun in his hand and yelling at me, "You are killing me and I might as well be dead." If he couldn't have me, no one else could. Our marriage was over and it was a hard blow to him. The reality is, it was over far before this Father's Day morning.

It is only now as I reflect on those 20 prior years that I was able to see the signs. They were there all along. Concealed behind the bushes at the intersection. Hidden in plain sight. Then BAM! You hear the crash of metal. The unexpected collision (hindsight is 20/20).

The reality is, I don't know if I ever was "in love" with him or just the thought of "being in love" I tried to make things "work" and stayed in the relationship far too long. It is only now I know the harm I did to my children. I taught my daughter it was okay for a woman to be verbally and mentally belittled and abused as her father did to her mother. I also taught my son it was permissible to mistreat a woman, the way his father mistreated his mother.

Our only form of communication was arguing. I was fed lies one manipulative spoonful after another. This was not a home to raise children in. Children thrive better with parents living separately with two happy parents than together in one home full of misery. That Father's Day morning was the shocking evidence of how dangerous holding on to a fraying rope can be.

I carried no visible bruises and had no broken bones. I had scars, scars so deep no one could see. The scars were hidden in my spirit. I silently cried for help, not with words. I hurt myself. Not with pills or cuts, but with food. I tried to sooth my feelings with food, much as my mother did when I was young. I weighed 425 pounds at that time. I used my weight as my armor like a "cloak of invisibility." No one wants to be near a fat woman and I didn't need to worry about leaking my story. I realized I was only hurting me; the outside of me was simply a reflection of the pain inside me.

Standing at the bathroom mirror, I found myself staring at a stranger. Someone who looked familiar, yet unknown. Reflecting on yesterday and finally having a tomorrow to dream for myself. I was free of all the roles I needed to fill for everyone else but me. As a painter looking at a blank canvas with joy and anticipation seeing their result, before they even pick up a brush, the masterpiece is imagined. I was now a blank canvas; I was now the artist holding the brush. I was lost… Where do I start?

Knowing who I WAS NO LONGER was evident. I knew I needed to heal from all my past traumas. I put in the work; I knew if I didn't, I wasn't going to make it. I worked with a therapist on a weekly basis. During that time, I was also studying to become a Life/Health coach and later becoming a Transformational coach. The deep work began, the deep reflections of my life. I realized I was asking the universe for exactly what I was receiving. After all, nothing changes if nothing changes. How do I make the change I want to be? How do I change?

I was reading, and later studied the Hawaiian practice of Ho'oponopono (basically meaning to correct or make right), an ancient transformational technique.

The forgiveness prayer is said with your eyes closed as a meditation as you say,

I am sorry

Please forgive me

Thank you

I love you

Telling myself I was sorry was hard. Asking ME to forgive myself—DAMN! What did I need to ask myself for forgiveness for? I finally realized the need to do so, and I had to forgive myself for allowing myself to be abused. I could have gotten out of the cycle at any time; however, I chose to stay. I thanked myself for the lessons learned, making the foundation to build on every day.

I love you.

Man, that was the hardest of all! I know I have the right to love and to be loved, but first I needed to learn to love the most important person … ME!

That's where the rubber hit the road. Back to coach training. With the aid of a fellow coaching student, we delved deeper into my childhood. I visited the younger me (the age when I was referred to by the nickname of Miffy). I started using my birthname of Mary-Frances during the transformation. I kneeled next to Miffy, looking her in the eye and asking her what was going on and engaged in conversations. Seems silly to hear, but it works!

During the conversations, I found my present self, Mary-Frances, becoming more confident and surer footed as Miffy felt safer and more assured.

The greatest gift during my healing journey was the bond between me and my grandson. He spent the summer with me before he started kindergarten. Unknown adventures lay ahead and he was apprehensive about this new experience and Mary-Frances was able to have open conversations with him. I held a safe space for:

Thoughts: Am I going to know anyone? How will I make friends? What if the teacher is mean?

Feelings: I am scarred that no one will like me. I am afraid I will get lost.

We addressed his concerns, one by one in great depth. I provided words of encouragement; ironically, the words Miffy needed to hear at his age and sadly did not.

This was my beginning.

Mary-Frances Buckland

Mary-Frances Buckland is a Transformational Health and Life Coach specializing in healing wounds from the past empowering a self-actualized future. She is also a certified Reiki therapist, hypnotherapist, a certified mastermind leader, a teacher for 18 years, beekeeper, and an ordained minister. As a public speaker, she has graced the stage at Secret Knock, a Forbes, Inc., and Entrepreneur top-rated event.

Mary-Frances' career evolved from her life experiences. The proud mother of two children, her marriage ended in divorce. Afterward, she rebounded from one relationship, a pattern that would repeat itself until she realized that the universe was giving her just what she was asking for. After the passing of her parents, Mary-Frances began her journey of self-discovery as she studied to become a health, life, and transformational coach. It was during that time she realized she needed to heal from her past before she felt confident to help others. Unraveling years of abuse and neglect required forgiveness and a deep study into real and perceived emotions. Putting everything in God's hands, her healing took her on the path to help others.

Today, Mary-Frances coaches the homeless to find value in themselves as well as self-worth. This work has been a work of God as He guided her to do His work through her.

Connect with Mary-Frances at www.MaryFrancesBuckland.com.

CHAPTER 14

Bold Risks Are Small Choices

Niki Hall

"Don't be afraid to give up the good to go for the great."
~John D. Rockefeller

Don't be afraid to take the risk to move your life from good to great. That quote is not an easy thing to live by. A long time ago, between the ages of four to eight, I had this continuous "Why?" going off in my mind. I was trying to understand what people were talking about and why they would do certain things. I was constantly trying to figure too much out.

Let me tell you, you really don't know how to put much together at that age. No way could I answer those beyond me "Why?" questions that I was consistently asking myself or others. That question was my constant companion. Because I couldn't seem to figure anything out and because I was always playing with kids older than me, my first reaction, even when playing a game of hide and seek, was to … cry. Yup! I'd cry. I would beg the bigger and older kids to let me play. Convince them I could, then when they allowed me to join them, for all sorts of reasons; they picked me, they didn't pick me, they ran too fast, I couldn't do it as well as the others, pick a circumstance and it would make me cry.

That really wasn't much fun. I had to start figuring out some of my own important "Why?" questions. Once I realized I could make my own choices about things, my little life became a lot easier. This is also when I realized that with choices came consequences, a kid's version of understanding risk and reward and the price that may come with it. And so, there it is. I became a little risk-taker in the making. This is the manner of living I chose then and still live by now. It seemed best for my character and that "Why?" questioning that always went off in my mind would end up serving me very well. With this new discovery, I had to learn how to fit in, be myself and achieve my goals.

That went on for about four more years, when I had to transition into high school, and that led me to face myself again. I was at a crossroads. I had to take a big risk, one way or the other, to tell my parents what I was interested in or to conform and follow the masses. Both directions had results that I would have to live with for a long time, possibly have regret and keep going in that direction once I was out of high school, never knowing if I would ever be able to make a come back in the direction of my real life or not. That was my preteen thinking, "If I don't speak up, I could be doomed forever."

I decided to speak up for myself. First to my mother, I told her even though no girl is doing it yet, I want to study in the tech wing in high school. I didn't want to learn business. I asked my mother for permission to go talk to the councillor in the high school to help me figure out how to get in the tech wing. My mother gave me permission, so now I wasn't wrecking my future. Instead, I put myself on the line as the first girl to walk into the tech wing. The school agreed to let me take technical classes instead of business classes.

During the next four years, I was honing my skills at identifying risks in this new environment, which there were many. Sometimes I felt like I had no choice but to pick the less torturous direction because every direction I was faced with had risk. I had to prioritize my goal, the risk, then learn to look past it, and toward what would be a big reward for me, as long as I would keep seeing these challenges to the end.

"If you are going through hell, keep going."
~Winston Churchill

Follow through was hard at times, but well worth the effort, and I knew it. I would analyze the risks and behaviors that had to go with them and I gave it everything I got. I'm sure at times I looked a little abrupt or very forward. I was trying to implement a direction to a solution and I hadn't developed good habits or a character that wouldn't get you to notice my persistence or habit that's slightly different from the others. I found it was not an easy thing to do, being different, wanting to fit in, and felt the effects of peer pressure.

As if I wasn't piling enough on myself at the time already, during those same years I was developing a self-awareness. It showed me that although my friends and fellow students accepted me, I wasn't really cut out for small city living. I came to the conclusion that if I married a "big city guy" that this choice would suit me best. Again, my self-identity was at risk. More small choices to lead to a big reward. These choices to create a big result had to run simultaneously parallel with the growth and personal development I was working on as a girl in the tech wing at high school. The risk this time was leaving my family and friends. The reward was finding my soul mate, which I did and I did.

I lived through so many identities or parts of myself during that time in my life; a daughter, a sister, a friend, a wife, a self-employed contractor, and a mother. I loved all of my roles and I was able to do it with confidence and eventually an ease and flow had developed from all my small choices for the roles I played in my life. I lived this life without reservation for decades. I really can honestly say I have no regrets. Living a Big Risk, Big Rewards manner of living is an effective way to becoming your real self, without reservation or regret. This is true!

That phase of my life is behind me now and once more the time had come where a new search of myself was facing me. I decided to give all my wisdom, dedication and all that I have come to know away by means of becoming a Mindset and Success Coach. I've taken many risks and small choices to get here. I tested the market for myself, saw I could do it; this new business and I hung a shingle. For now, I understand how to recognize risks, weigh the pros and cons, put the risk into a priority state, create and implement results from all the small choices to get to the big result, implement that plan, monitor my move forward and reap the big rewards. Also, I do recognize now that all the fun is in making those choices, facing those challenges and taking the next steps forward. This is where a lot of my life's pleasures ended up stemming from.

Through the teachings of master thinkers that I've learnt, the application I have put into my own work, I have broken through that low 20% of the population that shares that fraction of a business's income. I am now living a happy, fulfilling life while I am on my way to living more joyous, more happiness, and more fulfilling times ahead.

With that understanding, the Big Risk was my not becoming who I was determined to be, and the big reward is my being able to stay on this life learning journey for all of my life. The result is that now I give more than I get and that pleases me beyond measure.

If I were to speak to a student of mine at this present time of story sharing, I would say something like, "It's time to be honest with yourself. Ask yourself the hard questions. And be who you think you are whatever that be. If you're thinking of something, other people are thinking of the same thing.

"You don't have to make big decisions with drastic changes. I would like to encourage you to recognize and accept what is best for you. Start to recognize and eliminate old habits so you can replace them with new habits. We are all aware of the difference one degree can make. So start with just that if you must. Making one change of a habit causes a one-degree change in your personal growth and goal trajectory.

"Understand that this life is not a trial run. This is the only life you'll get. Be who you organically are meant to be, who you have always been. I assure you that you can't go wrong being and believing in yourself. This is your time to shine, your time to take the big risks, a ton of small choices that will get you to you. So, you too can reap the big reward, by being yourself!"

Niki Hall

Niki Hall is a Mindset and Success Coach .

Realizing her personal ability to help people, she opened a self-help school. She later wrote a book entitled, *Building Up - Thoughts Expressed During the Readjustment of Self*, a book on Change and Self-Actualization, where her first printing sold out within days of its release. This catapulted her into public speaking and workshop engagements.

In 2023, Niki published three #1 bestselling author stories that shed light on manners of growth and your ability to further establish attitudes for personal gain.

Niki has hung a shingle out to inspire entrepreneurs take action, increase their lifestyle, and achieve their full potential. The ultimate goal is to provide information to individuals in reaching more prosperity in their health, wealth or business, through the better understanding and application of mindset.

Connect with Niki on Facebook @niki.hall.148.

CHAPTER 15

We Will No Longer Use You

Norm Hull

To the people in my life who see, appreciate, and support
me. My life is better because of all of you.

"We will not be using your services for our programs this summer."

Seventeen years of dedication to an organization, only to be handed a pink slip with an unexpected dismissal. It stung—a contradictory blow to the commitment I'd poured into the institution. According to the head of the organization, I seemed "tired," lacking the necessary "energy" for the role. It felt like getting kicked to the curb, undeservedly so.

Yet, amidst the disappointment, irony lurked. The person delivering the news was unaware of the board's intentions to replace them—a position I'd advocated to keep them in. But here I was, deemed expendable.

The initial shock led to a determination not to be defined by this setback. While others simmered in anger and resentment, I focused on carving out a new path. Vacuums, after all, need to be filled, and if I did not fill it myself, someone else could dictate my future. In this moment I was realizing one of the conditions of that happening.

The shock, anger and feeling of betrayal that was attached to the moment when my connection with the organization was severed was hard to move past. From both perspectives of the principals involved, it was a bitter lesson about trust, insecurity, and self-preservation.

Have you ever felt like the value you provide just becomes an afterthought?

In one of the many moments of introspection that I had after the declarations was recognizing how easy it is to have another person determine your value and the battle you need to take on to fight the story they are trying to sell you about you!

My career was at risk, and I decided to take action to ensure that I, not someone else, determined my path forward.

How many stories have we heard about others getting to a place in their life where they reached their line in the sand where they would no longer let their suggestions, ideas and evolutionary concepts be ignored, overlooked or discounted by another? I was there but I did not get to this place on my own volition: it was a place where someone else brought me.

You arrive at this place in your life and you either resent the person who brings you there or you can realize this is an unexpected, or desired opportunity for you to shine. It is much easier to say, write and conceptually consider with time.

My Big Risk opportunity was not at the time of my choosing but it had arrived. It could have been pure luck or just time. You usually do not have the luxury of picking your opportunities, but you need to be ready when they arrive.

My Big Risk was providing me the opportunity to create my own table and not hope for a seat at someone else's.

Thus, I embarked on my Big Risk: creating my summer leadership program.

With limited capital and a ticking clock, I rallied friends and disenchanted clients to my cause. Doubts loomed large, but with unwavering support and determination, we pressed on.

Taking the risk provided so many benefits and new components to my business that exceeded the initial action of creating my own leadership program.

We now offer another way to develop leaders in a marketplace that has used the same process for decades. Our ability to offer the tools, techniques and fresh processes has created a magnet that draws in clients better aligned with our perspective on leadership.

One of the rewards that has helped heal my heart is valuing our staff. They are not 'hired' from elsewhere and 99% are past participants. Our program is designed to let the talent of others shine, suggest new areas to address, and a commitment to enhancing their skills. I do not expect them to stay with the program forever, and when they do move forward toward achieving their dreams, goals and aspirations, they find support.

The results spoke volumes.

My business expanded, and speaking invitations and the number of events I created multiplied. Each one became easier and broadened the topics I was teaching. Because of my events, financial rewards and returns, I have more freedom. Thirty-three years later, our program thrives, enriching minds and coffers alike. The number of people influenced by the content, teachings and experiences we have provided is over 30,000 attendees.

But the best personal reward? The freedom to chart my own course, to prove that setbacks are merely steppingstones to success.

Yet, amidst the triumph, one tale stands out: a mindset that limits and a concept that most people miss, but if you can overcome it, you will find Big Rewards in the life you lead.

It has become an anecdote of shortsightedness that cost a prestigious college dearly.

Hosting an event at said institution, we fell short of our attendance projections. No matter, I thought—a minor blip in an otherwise successful endeavor. But our contact had other ideas, insisting on a hefty attrition fee.

The irony was palpable. The previous year, we'd exceeded our reserved space by 50, without so much as a whisper because the college collected and appreciated the additional revenue. But a shortfall of 25 attendees, and suddenly, it was open season on our wallets.

I attempted to reason with our contact, to appeal to their sense of fairness. But it was like teaching a goldfish to tap dance—futile and bewildering.

Ultimately, we took our business elsewhere the next year—a decision that cost the college dearly. Over the years, they missed almost a million dollars in site fees, because of a staff member's short-sightedness.

Yet, from their oversight, a valuable lesson emerged: never let the narrow-mindedness of others determine your destiny. When faced with adversity, seize the opportunity to forge your own path—and watch as setbacks transform into triumphs.

Here are additional lessons learned over the years from taking that Big Risk and I have incorporated into my Philosophy on Life (POL)

- **A Risk Can Be a Personal Development Leapfrog:**
  - I went from being just another hired speaker headlining someone else's events to creating my own. Let me tell you, it was like going from an extra in a movie to the leading role. As a result of expanding my business model, I could bypass decision makers and event planners who viewed me and my peers as commodities. It's funny how what seemed like being pushed over a cliff now looks more like a diving expedition where I found buried treasure. Lesson learned: don't waste time convincing others of your worth when you can invest energy in dazzling the world with your talent instead.
  - Question: Who's failing to see your shine, and you are trying to help them have better eyesight?

- **Embracing the Exit:**
  - Getting the boot from an organization usually comes with a side order of anger, hurt, and a sprinkle of betrayal. But why waste emotions on a company picnic when they don't want you to attend or stay? Turn those feelings into internal fuel for your future endeavors. Getting mad is normal, justified, and part of the grieving process, but don't let it turn into a permanent state of mind.
  - Question: Which emotion is gatekeeping your ticket to your Bold Risk-Big Reward fine dining experience?

- **Zoom Out, Gain Clarity:**
  - Sometimes we get so caught up in the pixelated details that we forget to step back and admire the masterpiece. Looking at the bigger picture isn't just about finding Waldo; it's about realizing that the whole canvas is your playground. Investing in the panoramic view pays better dividends than

obsessing over individual brushstrokes. So, take a step back, grab binoculars, and marvel at the landscape of your dreams.

- Question: If hindsight were a time machine, how would you tweak your current dream-chasing strategy? What's the Big Risk waiting for you to give it the green light?

There is no guarantee if you take a Big Risk, it will favor you and the outcome will be profitable or personally rewarding.

The risk I share here was in the context of an income stream being dammed up, an opportunity that was present and no one was taking advantage of, and someone limiting my skills and talent. These conditions made it a no-brainer to take that leap of faith and bet on myself.

Being told I was not going to be '*used*' was received as one of the biggest disappointments in my life. Ultimately, however, it was one of the best things to happen because of my risk taking.

The Big Risk was creating my event. Still, an even more significant risk is staying in a situation where you are not seen, appreciated or given an opportunity to share your talents with the world.

You will find it is the person you view in the mirror who is the one you need to show your true potential and convince to take that Big Risk. The transformation within will be your Big Reward.

Norm Hull

Norm Hull is a force to be reckoned with in leadership consulting and speaking. As the principal owner of Norm Hull & Associates, his innovative and thought-provoking presentations have captivated audiences worldwide for over 38 years.

Norm's impact extends far and wide, having trained thousands of youth leaders and adult professionals since 1980. His impressive list of educational institutions, associations, and corporate clients include Pepsico, Jostens, Herff Jones YUM, Taco Bell, National Association of Student Councils, YPO, DECA, FBLA, FFCLA, Pizza Hut, Fox Travel Inc, Disney, Universal Studios, Department of Defense, University of Mississippi, Tulane University, and many more.

Norm's passion for personal development has led him to author and co-author several books on leadership. His contribution to the individual development industry has benefited over 3,000,000 audience members and clients across all 50 states in America, as well as in Russia, Canada, Spain, Costa Rica, Finland, England, Germany, Bahrain, Kuwait, and several other Middle Eastern countries.

Norm earned a Certified Speaking Professional (CSP) designation through the National Speakers Association. His high-energy facilitation skills are particularly sought after for high-stakes meetings, national and international conferences, and other events that require an engaging leadership expert.

Norm Hull is an acclaimed speaker and leadership expert who consistently delivers thought-provoking, interactive, and inspirational presentations. Norm Hull is a true difference-maker in every sense of the word.

Connect with Norm at www.TalentAdvantages.com.

CHAPTER 16

Finding Love Again: My Journey to a Second Chance

Pam Langord

To Bill. You are my penguin.

I've never been a risk-taker, always preferring the safety of predictability. But my cautious nature stemmed from years spent in the shadow of fear.

You see, for 25 years, I was married to an alcoholic. The last decade of our marriage was a constant battle against the mind-numbing fear— fear of exposure, fear of loss, fear of the unknown. Every choice I made was dictated by this all-encompassing terror. As my husband's addiction spiraled out of control, so did his behavior.

The day that changed everything started innocuously—with a phone call from my husband's boss asking if he was okay. Unbeknownst to me, my husband had been calling in sick frequently, and I had no idea. Alarmed and feeling a queasy knot in the pit of my stomach, I headed home early.

As I pulled up, the sight of the open garage and the sounds of my dogs' frantic barking filled me with dread. My heart pounded as I rushed inside, only to be hit by the smell of something burning. In the kitchen, a forgotten pot was scorching on the stove, smoke filling the air. And there, oblivious to the danger, was my husband, passed out on the couch.

In that moment, a tidal wave of emotions overwhelmed me—relief that I had arrived in time, rage at his reckless disregard for our safety, and a bone-deep panic about what could have happened. That day marked the beginning of the end.

The divorce process was a brutal, soul-crushing experience. Each day brought new challenges and emotional turmoil. I felt as though I was drowning in a sea of paperwork, legal battles, and the wreckage of my once-shared life. The fear that had been my constant companion for so long now threatened to swallow me whole.

I questioned my own worth, my judgment, and my ability to create a future for myself. The life I had built, the identity I had crafted, crumbled around me. I was left raw, exposed, and utterly terrified of what lay ahead. In my heart of hearts, I knew I would never be able to trust again, to open my heart completely to another. I had been through too much and carried too many scars. So, I retreated into myself, building walls around my battered heart, determined to protect myself from ever feeling that pain again.

One thing that helped keep me sane even in the darkest times was food. I found solace in my kitchen. Cooking has always been a passion of mine, a way to express my creativity and feel grounded. Even as my world fell apart, I continued to pour my heart into my cooking. It gave me a sense of normalcy when my life was anything but.

I started sharing my kitchen creations on Facebook with friends and family, posting what I lovingly call food porn. It was a way for me to connect with others and share an undamaged piece of myself. Little did I know, my posts would become the catalyst for a life-changing reconnection.

Walking away from my marriage left me trembling with fear of the unknown. As I navigated the challenges of divorce and approached my 50th birthday, I made a vow to myself: no more risks. I had taken enough leaps of faith to last a lifetime. I was too old to start over.

My post-divorce plan was simple: I would be the eccentric lady on the hill with her beautiful dogs, finding joy in her garden, cooking gourmet meals and pouring her heart into her work. I would be content in my own company, free from the threat of heartbreak.

But life has a way of surprising us, and fate has a crazy sense of humor...

There is a quote I love from the Princess Diaries that has always resonated with me.

"Courage is not the absence of fear but rather the
judgment that something is more important than fear."
~Princess Diaries

I wouldn't call myself courageous, but the idea of prioritizing something above fear strikes a chord. I tell you all of this because this is a love story. My love story.

Once upon a time, a 15-year-old girl served as a bridesmaid at her favorite sister's wedding. She had never met her escort, the groom's youngest brother Bill, yet from that very first moment it was as if they had known each other all their lives. They spent the entire event whispering, laughing and offering snarky commentary. They danced every dance and spent every moment that they could. It was as if their souls recognized they belonged with each other.

But despite their best efforts, timing, distance, and the follies of youth conspired against them.

In an era before cell phones and social media (gasp, I'm that old!), maintaining a relationship across the miles proved challenging. But no matter when or where we saw each other, every reunion felt like coming home, and I found myself falling deeper in love each time.

Bill and I danced in and out of each other's lives through high school and college, never quite finding our rhythm or revealing the depth of our feelings for each other. Without something to tether us, we eventually drifted apart and went our separate ways. I married and moved away, and he moved on as well. Though we occasionally caught glimpses of each other's lives through shared relatives, we completely lost touch.

Years later, fate brought us face to face at our niece's graduation party. I have to admit to being nervous when I found out he was attending. It had been years. What did he look like? What would he think of me?

When he walked through the door, time stood still as if it were in suspended animation. I would've recognized him anywhere. It was just like always. We started talking and laughing as if no time had passed. In all honesty, all I remember of that evening was Bill. And I'd be lying if I didn't admit there was a tinge of longing that filled my heart wondering what might have been. But with both of us married, it was just a beautiful moment in time to cherish.

Fast forward through my personal hell, as I fought through the throes of divorce. It was a simple Facebook post about one of my kitchen creations that prompted Bill to reach out, asking if I truly cooked all those meals myself.

My heart skipped a beat.

With a simple "Yes," the floodgates opened, and we found ourselves texting into the wee hours of the morning, night after night. He learned of my impending divorce, and I discovered that he was facing the end of his marriage, too. We discovered we had suffered in similar ways over the years. We had both been deeply wounded by those closest to us, retreating into ourselves for protection.

I was resolute in my desire to never again expose myself to such pain. The idea of opening up, of risking my heart once more, filled me with bone-deep terror. I had my plan—I would be the eccentric dog lady, living on the hill.

But remember what I said about fate's sense of humor?

Days into our rekindled connection, Bill took a leap of his own. He confessed that he was falling for me all over again.

I was stunned.

I could go with my plan and play it safe, where we remain Facebook friends and nothing more.

But something long forgotten stirred within me...

Instead of retreating to the safety of my carefully constructed walls, I gathered every ounce of courage I possessed. With a deep breath and a trembling heart, I admitted that I, too, was falling. I chose to take the leap.

That was over eight years ago. Eight years filled with more love, laughter, and genuine support than I have ever known. This man, my soulmate and partner, has become my safe haven. Every day I give thanks for the courage we both showed in that pivotal moment. We recognized that the potential of our love was greater than the fear of being hurt.

Looking back, I see how much I've grown and learned about love, happiness, and myself. I now know that it's never too late for a second chance, no matter how broken you may feel. There is always hope for a brighter future.

If you are reading this and you are struggling, feeling lost, or alone, please hear me: your story isn't over. Your happy ending is waiting for you. Don't be afraid to take a chance on love, on happiness, and on yourself.

When my own second chance arrived, I almost let it pass me by. I nearly allowed fear to rob me of the greatest love of my life. But by taking that leap of faith, I discovered a love that heals, a love that empowers, a love that makes me feel truly alive.

Embrace your second chances. Trust in the journey. And always remember that you are worthy of love, just as you are.

Pam Langord

Pam Langord is a seasoned strategist who blends practical insights with innovative approaches for scaling online businesses. Through her proprietary MAGIC framework, Pam combines traditional marketing strategies with cutting-edge AI, leveraging technology and data to drive sustainable business growth. With decades of experience, she simplifies the tech landscape for entrepreneurs, offering tailored solutions that focus on tangible results—where magic meets metrics.

Pam's journey is marked by a transformative personal story. After navigating a turbulent marriage, she channeled her resilience into founding her own business, a step that not only provided her with safety but also unleashed her professional creativity. This personal revolution has enhanced her empathy and effectiveness, allowing her to guide other entrepreneurs through their unique challenges with a deep understanding and compassion.

When she's not geeking out on new technology or helping clients find freedom in their businesses, you'll find Pam in the kitchen getting her foodie on or shamelessly posting food porn and puppy pics.

Whether it's in the kitchen or in the market, Pam is about transforming challenges into opportunities, ensuring her clients—and she herself—continuously grow and thrive.

Connect with Pam at https://pamlangord.com.

CHAPTER 17
Sharing With the Nations

Romy Faith Ganser

I would like to dedicate my chapter to my family and friends who have lifted me when I was down and held on tight to keep me there. Much love to you.

"If you see something … Say something … If you hear something … Say something."

It was February 2005. I was standing in front of a group of people in a hotel meeting room. The presenter was Christian Prophet David Wagner instructing us all on how to listen when the Holy Spirit speaks to us.

Again, he said softly and gently … "If you see something … Say something. If you hear something … Say something."

I had been chosen to be the subject. They were tuning in on me. One man stood, "I see you wearing magnificent blessings, necklaces of gems and pearls." A woman stood and said that she saw me in an abundant apple orchard and then she saw me entering a peach orchard inside the apple orchard that was overflowing with ripe fruit. Several more people shared their messages and to each one, I gave a nod and a thank you.

Then David turned to me and said, "Dear Sister, Romy, the Lord our God is showing favor on you. Favor upon you as He sees your struggles and yet you persevere. He hears the cries of your heart and he wants you to know he will reward your selflessness with much glory." Then he looked into my eyes and said, "I hear the Lord telling me that you will be sharing your story with many nations. You will do this and inspire others to overcome."

"Really?" I was thinking while trying to not look skeptical.

At that point in my life, I was in pain, both physically and emotionally. I had been recently divorced, had lost my brother to Leukemia, had been diagnosed with Multiple Sclerosis (MS) and Chronic Lyme Disease, sold the house that I loved and moved home with my young son, I had severe back pain from multiple falls and was unemployed … again. This had all happened in the previous five years AND He sees me speaking to nations?

I spent the next ten years coming to grips with this MS; what it meant for me and how best to live my life through it. I had battled to convince doctors that the pain in my back was not MS nerve pain. I was told more than once, "You have MS, Honey, your back is going to hurt." They wouldn't consider the life I had before MS. The years of working in hotels and restaurants, falling in kitchens. I was always pushing my body beyond its limits. Then there was the fall which led to an MRI and the diagnosis that changed it all.

It was a beautiful sunny Friday morning in June 2002. I got to work early and decided to treat myself to a large, iced hazelnut coffee and a blueberry muffin from the Dunkin' next door. I made my purchase and as I headed out a gentleman held the first door for me. I thanked him, turned, caught my foot under the mud mat, and slammed into the exterior door. I grabbed for the door handle with the hand holding the coffee and hit my head wrenching my neck while breaking my shoulder on the door frame. I wound up half in and half out the door with my sundress around my waist, wearing my coffee and lying on my muffin.

Two weeks later, my hand started to go numb. The young Orthopedic doctor who ordered my MRI couldn't look at me as he delivered the news. He said, "You've done a lot of falling over the years, Romy. Your spine looks like that of a Rugby Player, but we can't worry about that now. You have MS."

This was not the first time a doctor had mentioned Multiple Sclerosis. Since college, I had neurological episodes from spasms and numbness in my legs to short-term memory lapses and cognition issues. I even had my bunions operated on at 24 years old because my feet would get numb while working in heels. These issues were so intermittent that doctors never considered MS to be the cause.

This confirmed diagnosis set off a series of events. The first doctor I consulted with was referred to me by a doctor with MS. He started with, "Well, you'll be in a wheelchair in five years." He went on to say that I was done having kids. He would start me on a chemo and steroid treatment. I would lose my hair. And it could open me up to the chances of Leukemia. His bedside manner left something to be desired, but he was the doctor that doctors went to, right?

Soon after, my mother met a girl who had been treated for MS before they found that she actually had Chronic Lyme Disease. I consulted with her doctor and found that I did indeed have this Chronic Disease. The next Doctor ordered a spinal tap to positively confirm the MS diagnosis. When reporting the findings, he was sure that I had traveled to the UK. I laughed and said I had never been out of the US.

Six months of IV antibiotics found me with more energy and less fogginess in my head. More importantly, though, was that another MRI showed the shading on my spine had cleared. No scars on the spine, but several scars on the nerves in my brain remained.

I still wasn't feeling great, so I consulted a Naturopath. This doctor started taking my medical history, then stopped and said, "They have great results with bee sting therapy for MS." I laughed, which confused her. I told her that I was allergic to bee stings. I went on to say that when I was ten years old I had been stung on the top of my head by a European hornet. It dropped me to my knees and I nearly died. We had an exterminator come out who confirmed that these hornets were extremely aggressive. There was an aha moment before the doctor declared that was how I had gotten Lyme Disease. Yes, from a bee sting. I had a rare European strain of Lyme Disease that I had carried in my system for 25 years. And that underlying virus was the cause of my MS.

With the Lyme Disease under control and my MS treatment well underway, I needed to find a job. Still suffering from back pain, I walked with two canes or a walker. I had many great interviews but did not receive callbacks. I even landed freelance work that would end due to no fault of my own. I didn't know what to do. Where to go. I was at a loss.

At the end of the Covid shutdown, I finally had back surgery and needed to get out and keep moving. I started walking with Sally Green, the Vice President of Action Takers Publishing, and a friend I hadn't seen since our grown kids were in youth group together. As we walked and talked, I shared my story. She told me she was working on a collaborative book called *Wellness For Winners* and that I "needed to be in it!" I had done some writing before and had belonged to a memoir writing group, but I had never imagined publishing a story … *MY story*.

I would have to make an investment in me, emotionally and financially. I wasn't sure I could do it. I prayed. Then I prayed some more. Then I did it! I reached out to Lynda Sunshine West, the President of Action Takers Publishing, and the journey began!

When my chapter was edited, it needed one comma. Woohoo, I had always been an avid reader and always had a red pen nearby to correct the editor's mistakes.

When the book launched on Amazon, it instantly became a bestseller, and I became a #1 International Bestselling Author! I went on to publish a chapter in a second book called *The Book I Read*. I wrote about some life experiences I had while reading the Bible. This book, too, instantly became a bestseller!

Soon after the launch of the second book, Lynda Sunshine reached out to me to ask if I would like to proofread some of her upcoming books. I was delighted when six months later, Lynda Sunshine shared that she would like to focus more on the marketing and sales portion of her business and would like me to be her Editor in Chief for Action Takers Publishing.

What an amazing experience this has been; meeting new people from around the world, editing their stories to make them shine, working a job I love, from home, at my pace, in my own time, at a job that I did not have to walk into an interview for.

AND I have shared my story with the nations over and over again!

For I know the plans I have for you, declares the LORD,
plans to prosper you and not to harm you, plans to give you
hope and a future. ~Jeremiah 29:11

Romy Faith Ganser

Romy Faith Ganser is a freelance editor, proofreader, ghostwriter, public speaker, devoted mom, daughter, sister, and lover of Jesus Christ. Besides working on her own projects, she has worked on over 20 books for Action Takers Publishing.

When not working with Action Takers Publishing, Romy is a Professional Event Planner. Having attended Johnson and Wales University, she spent 20 years in the hospitality industry, honing her skills in every facet of the business. When her body couldn't do the on-site tasks anymore, Romy turned to specializing in Sales, Marketing, and administrative event planning duties.

Romy's gift is in focusing on the little details while looking at the overall project. In editing, it may be assisting an author in creating a piece that best reflects their true self. In event planning, she attends to the little things that make the perfect celebration for your big day.

Romy loves to keep moving. She spends time flat water kayaking, low-impact yoga-ing, working out at the gym, lifting, spinning, and kicking it at boot camp. Romy loves to write and has always had a book or two or three nearby.

Romy has conquered numerous challenges over the last 20 years. Her goal is to continue to persevere and spread light and love to those around her.

Romy would be delighted to discuss your projects and see how she might help you shine.

Connect with Romy at https://Linktr.ee/RomyFaith.

CHAPTER 18

Life Adventures for the Benefit of Others

S. Kay McBreairty

Mom and Dad, thank you for giving me the genes of courage and adventure with integrity of purpose.

On August 31, 1988, nearing the end of Summer in the Allagash feels like Fall. My sister Peggy's home is warm in temperature and more so in spirit.

"Seattle is so far away." "Look at you so young and beautiful and venturing out on your own." "Aren't there jobs in Maine?" "You'll need to visit often." "I know you'll do well." Various comments at my farewell party. So much love and support. I drove off the next day with a hug from my brother Phil and his words, "I'll miss you more than you know," weighing heavy on my heart. Leaving family wasn't easy.

Looking back, I am glad I had the gumption—not to move 3,000 miles away from home—but to start a new chapter in my life pursuing my dreams. They weren't so stupendous that I couldn't reach them by living closer to family.

But I had fallen in love with the Pacific Northwest when I was stationed there in the U.S. Air Force. It was like the Allagash countryside but bigger—mountains, rivers, trees .... Nature is such a huge part of my spirituality (perhaps the Irish in me), and I have an adventurous spirit in my blood.

"Look how organized her vehicle is," Mom says showing her sister Ruth the inside of my Chevy S10 Blazer. It's clean, full of gas, and sitting ominously in the dooryard as the hours near for my departure.

Then off I go driving by myself all the way across the country in the days before there were cell phones. It scares me today just thinking about it. Youth. We don't always know what to be afraid of, and that can be good or bad. But in this case, it worked out with just a few bumps in the road.

While I had no place to live when I reached the Seattle area, I had a few friends in the area from when I was stationed at McChord Air Force Base in Tacoma. They each gave me a bed for a few days, and that took care of me for a couple of weeks.

Within that time, I learned that a cousin from Maine lived in Federal Way, and we agreed to move to a larger apartment unit and share rent. Place to live; check.

As I had been a certified paralegal in the Air Force, I went to headhunters to find a paralegal job in Seattle. Hmmmm, not so easy. My military lingo didn't quite translate – I was met with glazed over eyes when describing how my skills and experience matched their needs. But I was able to get a job with one of the law firms as a legal secretary. Job; check.

The Disabled American Veterans (DAV) organization paid the tuition for me to take classes at night to get a second certification as a paralegal, but this time from a civilian school. Then the law firm I was working for as a legal secretary gave me a paralegal job.

My career continuously progressed over the next 30 years, along with numerous successes with side businesses – selling jewelry, stitchery, cleaning products, car club membership, life insurance, the list goes on. What I considered rewards at the time I later came to realize didn't actually contribute to a meaningful life – an interesting one – perhaps an inspiring or accomplished one – but the meaningfulness and biggest reward came later.

The legal profession served me well. The first law firm in Seattle touted a prior governor in its ranks. It was the firm that first hired me as a legal secretary and later gave me the paralegal position.

The next law firm sent me to London for a month twice – I turned 30 in Mayfair. I even got to sit in one of the boxes at Lloyd's of London. I was awe inspired – a different country; a prestigious, historic, and international insurance company. I had arrived.

Next up was working for the Washington State Attorney General's Office in the capitol. I was the lead paralegal on the last two judicial hangings conducted in the United States. The level of responsibility was intense as I took the calls from the United States Supreme Court saying they wouldn't stay the executions.

I went to school at night again – this time for a bachelor's degree in organizational management. At graduation as Summe Cum Laude, my name was also called to receive an Integrity in Business award. While I have been known to say that my middle name is "Accountability," I hadn't realized my integrous nature shown through. It was a joyful day.

The degree opened other doors for me. I transitioned into the technology industry, even doing a stint at Boeing. Luckily, I secured a contract in California in the healthcare industry where I work today, as caring for children is special to my heart.

The bold risk of moving from Maine to Washington State when I separated from the military did provide big rewards careerwise. But the biggest reward is now.

I serve veterans as they transition from the military to ensure they thrive in the civilian workplace and their communities. And that came from my experience of what didn't work well when I first sought work in Seattle when I moved there from Maine in 1988.

I risked, and ultimately the biggest reward came now. Meaning in my life that brings me the most joy yet. Here's to your bold risks and realizing rewards specific to your heart's desires.

S. Kay McBreairty

S. Kay McBreairty is a professional Coach and Facilitator at Mc-Breairty – Reaching Your Potential. After working with individual clients for over two decades, she now works with groups that want to align their vocation with what matters most to them and contributes to their life mission.

As a United States Air Force veteran herself, Kay provides guidance to veterans of all military services in particular to ensure they thrive in the civilian workplace and communities when they transition from active duty. She wished the same types of services were available to her when she "got out" in relation to translating military skills and experience to the civilian job market, so she created that for others.

Kay finds providing encouragement and guidance accelerates one's forward movement to successful outcomes. For example, we don't need all of the answers to make progress. Kay can assist you in taking informed action and having confidence in your choices.

Connect with Kay at www.reachingyourpotential.world.

CHAPTER 19

Finding My Way Back: From Struggle to Strength

Shelly Snitko

Imagine standing on the edge of a cliff, the wind whipping against your face as you peer into the unknown depths below. Fear grips you, but deep down, there's a desire to take a chance and leap. The question is, will you? Will you summon the courage to jump, or will you remain paralyzed by fear?

Courage is not the absence of fear but rather learning to triumph over it. It's taking that leap even when you're afraid and every instinct screams at you to stay put. I know this firsthand from my own experience of jumping off a cliff in Mexico. It took a few attempts, but eventually I made the brave leap. I did it afraid, stepping outside my comfort zone and conquering the fear that held me back.

Change is an inevitable reality. Life presents challenges that evoke change which can be seen as either obstacles or opportunities. You get to choose. Will you have the courage to face the challenges head-on or remain gripped by fear? As Zig Ziglar says, "You must make the choice to take the chance if you want anything in life to change."

Storms in life are much like waves; some create gentle ripples, while others are disruptive and life-altering. Let me contrast two different storms in my own life. Both challenged me to respond and adapt. One was being caught in a rip current and the other was the sudden onset of a neuromuscular storm that affected my son.

Amid the tranquility of a snorkeling adventure in Hawaii, the sudden onset of a rip current shattered the peaceful serenity of the moment. It was a stark reminder of nature's unpredictable power, plunging us into a realm of uncertainty and fear. The panic that surged within me mirrored the overwhelming emotions I experienced upon receiving my son's neuromuscular disorder diagnosis years earlier. In both instances, the instinct to survive kicked in, urging me to take immediate action to protect myself and my loved ones.

As the rip current threatened to pull us further from shore, my initial response was to fight against the relentless pull of the water. Every fiber of my being screamed for safety, driving me to swim with all my might against the current. It was a futile effort, fueled by fear and desperation, reminiscent of my instinctual need to control and fix the situation when confronted with my son's diagnosis. In both cases, the initial impulse was driven by a primal urge to survive, even if it meant disregarding logic and reason.

However, just as in the rip current, where my husband's calm guidance redirected us to safety, seeking support became paramount in navigating the metaphorical storm of my son's diagnosis. Though I needed support and assistance, I found myself hesitating to reach out. The overwhelming responsibility of caregiving weighed heavily on me. Days blurred into months, and months became years. As I juggled the relentless demands of caregiving, my world was shrinking to the confines of our home. Each passing day brought a sense of isolation, the weight of responsibility bearing down on me like an unrelenting burden.

Despite my overwhelming exhaustion, the thought of reaching out for help felt like an admission of weakness or failure. I was exhausted but, quite honestly, I struggled in defining my needs and in knowing how to ask for help. The isolation grew as the demands of caring for our son consumed my time and energy, leaving little bandwidth for maintaining friendships or seeking support.

Navigating the uncertainty of both storms demanded a willingness to confront the unknown and relinquish the illusion of control. In the rip current, as I grappled with the relentless pull of the water, I was forced to confront my own vulnerability and surrender to the forces beyond my control. Similarly, facing my son's diagnosis required me to acknowledge my own limits and embrace the uncertainty of the future. In both instances, embracing vulnerability became the key to unlocking resilience and finding strength in the face of adversity.

Through the challenges posed by both storms, I learned invaluable lessons about resilience, adaptability, and the transformative power of vulnerability. I reached a pivotal moment six years ago. It was then that I realized the profound impact these challenges had on my life, propelling me towards a path of self-discovery and renewal.

Each step forward has been a testament to the unwavering courage that has propelled me through life's challenges, reaffirming my faith and belief in God's promises and his sustaining strength and grace.

Armed with courage and determination, I've leaned into the fear and confronted my inner demons head-on, peeling back the layers of self-doubt and negativity that had accumulated over the years. Fueled by a deep-rooted desire for change, I continue this transformative journey.

Guided by my faith and the unwavering support of loved ones, I am releasing the self-doubt and insecurity. It has been a journey marked by pivotal moments – from the realization of my own worth to the acceptance of vulnerability as a catalyst for growth.

Optavia's health program, my choice for addressing my weight gain, proved to be so much more than just another diet plan. The structure of the eating plan and the transformational system combined with my faith in God provided the scaffolding I needed to rebuild my life from the ground up. Through unwavering dedication and perseverance, I shed not only physical weight but also emotional baggage that had weighed me down for years. I learned to reframe my relationship with food, viewing it not as a source of comfort but as fuel for my body and soul.

This journey of transformation has been the catalyst in reclaiming my sense of self-worth, confidence, and purpose. As I shed the old habits and thought patterns that had held me back, I'm embracing a new way of living—one rooted in caring for myself as well as others. It demands continual shifts in mindset and behavior along with a willingness to embrace discomfort to facilitate growth and change. But it continues to be a journey of uncovering hidden strengths and rediscovering lost passions.

With newfound clarity and purpose, I stepped into my role as a health coach with Optavia, eager to empower others to prioritize their health and well-being. Unaware, this brave leap of starting my health coaching business is opening doors of opportunity I never imagined.

Drawing upon my own experiences and lessons learned along the way, my mission is to share my story with other family caregivers—to inspire, empower, and uplift those who may be struggling to find their way amid the relentless demands of caregiving. Through my work as a health coach and the founder of Caring For Me Too, I am committed to fostering a culture of nurturing self-care as a priority for all caregivers.

My passion is to help others find the courage to embrace change, face their fears head-on, and rise above adversity with renewed hope. It's only when we dare to venture outside our comfort zones, take bold risks, and embrace change, that we discover the true extent of our strength and potential.

Life is a journey, and each of us must navigate our own path through the storms that lie ahead. But no matter how fierce the winds may blow or how dark the skies may seem, know that you are not alone. Just like an eagle embraces storms, rising above them and soaring to new heights and emerges stronger, together we can confront the storms in our lives and find strength, renewal, and transformation.

Life's storms are inevitable, but they are not insurmountable. Dare to take bold risks in pursuit of your dreams. It may seem daunting, but it leads to big rewards. Isn't it time to uncover your true potential, soar to greater heights, and experience the joy that comes from facing life's challenges with courage and resilience?

Shelly Snitko

Shelly Snitko is an independent certified Optavia health coach, business leader, two-time international best-selling author, speaker, and founder of Caring For Me Too, a faith-based health and wellness community and caregiver coaching program.

She's been married to her college sweetheart, Chris Snitko, for over 40 years. They have two adult children, a son-in-love, four grandsons, and a granddaughter. Together they've created a life they love in Alabama.

As a business owner, wife, mom, nana, caregiver, friend, and mentor, she understands the many roles and daily demands of women. As veteran caregiver of their adult son with physical disabilities for over 28 years, she has navigated challenging life circumstances, loss, disappointment, and unrelenting responsibilities. She's experienced overwhelm and burnout caring for others' needs while neglecting her own.

Therefore, Shelly understands that 'caring for me too' isn't selfish, it's a necessity. Self-care doesn't put 'me first,' but prioritizes 'me too,' better equipped to care for loved ones as well as manage the stress and inevitable disappointments that caregivers encounter.

Her passion is empowering caregivers to live their best lives amid life's uncertainties and challenges. Caring For Me Too was birthed from personal experience of moving from surviving to thriving. With authentic vulnerability, she uplifts, inspires, encourages, and supports others toward whole health so they too can flourish.

Connect with Shelly at https://caringformetoo.com.

CHAPTER 20

WOW - There's a Story!

Sherri Leopold

To the Woman of Worth Warriors: your strength illuminates the path of self-empowerment. With unwavering courage, you forge ahead, inspiring and uplifting others. Your resilience is a beacon of hope helping every woman recognize her worth and Stand UP and Stand OUT as the unrepeatable miracle she is!

In February 2021, we were stuck in a time like we had never seen in recent history. While the pandemic was raging on, I was bursting with ideas. While driving home from an appointment, the radio station was sharing stories of black people in history. I pondered why aren't we talking about people who are alive and writing their own history? Don't people want to follow someone who is living?

I had an epiphany and wanted to highlight powerful black individuals who were writing and creating their own history. Bold move being a white woman interviewing black people. People asked me why I was doing it. I believed that we needed to show that, contrary to much of the media narrative, black people were not all criminals and in jail. I dove into my network and started asking people if they wanted to be part of what I called "Today's Black History Makers."

I started on February 13th and successfully interviewed 15 individuals. It was an incredibly rewarding experience. I enjoyed it so much that I told one of my friends that I mentor that I wished I'd had the bandwidth to do it all the way through women's history month, too. I was so excited to build this out bigger in 2022!

I started looking at 2022 candidates in late December and beginning of January. I opened my email and was greeted with an email that was asking if I wanted to be part of an advertising campaign that was the exact program I had done in February. The email came from one of the people I honored. I was so disappointed; I didn't have words. They simply rearranged the words and called it their own. I spent a couple of days sulking about what to do about it. When I shared with that friend what happened, he reminded me that I had the ability to do women's history month instead! I work with mostly women, so candidates would easily come to mind. I might have heard angels singing as the fog lifted and inspiration bloomed.

Working with strong, powerful women aligned with my Stop Self-Bullying Movement. I had heard the word WOW so many times during the writing of my book *Self-Bullying: What to do when the bully is YOU!* in 2018-19. WOW WARRIOR is someone who has learned to manage her own self-talk.

It was at that time that the word WOW evolved into its current meaning of *W.O.W. - Woman of Worth Warrior*. Prior to this, WOW was simply what people commonly said when hearing what self-bullying was. It was then that the WOW WARRIOR Award was born.

I spent the next few days developing the list of characteristics that a woman writing her own history would possess. Managing negative self-talk was the number one criterion. Also, they would have a network that would call them out if they self-bullied or needed encouragement. This woman would understand her worth, no matter her past experiences. She understands she is an inspiration and has one hand climbing up the ladder of success and one hand back to lift another sister up. She understands beyond a shadow of a doubt that she is an unrepeatable miracle and she is confident in her abilities without validation from anyone else.

She MUST give the award to herself knowing she is worthy.

THIS was a BIG RISK. I knew some women would refuse to do it. I stuck to my decision not knowing if I would be able to field enough women to make it work. I believed in my set of criteria, and worked until I had 31 candidates. I created the intro, the outro, recorded all the interviews and edited most everything myself. I created the promotional materials and took a risk and hired a full-time virtual assistant. She immediately integrated right into my idea and started helping with the promotion and all was going beautifully.

I proceeded to be absolutely amazed by the 31 women. We created an ebook and also scheduled a WOW WARRIOR Summit. To say that I was inspired by them would be a monumental understatement.

In fact, I was so inspired that I decided I wanted to develop and expand WOW WARRIOR into a full platform that included a magazine and a TV show of the same name. I began taping interviews like crazy and looking for writers and columnists, and also candidates for the WOW WARRIOR Award. Life was running at hyperspeed.

As I rounded out 2022, riding high on such an incredible year, and embarking on two new ventures, my world started to fall apart a little bit. My 95-year-old father-in-law who lived over three hours away started having problems which were causing major disruptions in our life. We tried to get him to move to an assisted living facility. When I should have been taping interviews and editing and all the things the WOW WARRIOR Platform required, I spent my time trying to get him to move. Then it all came crashing in and he wanted to move immediately. This required looking for places, meetings, renting trucks to move him, setting up his new place, etc. I was not consistent in coordinating the WOW WARRIORS of 2023. I only ended up with 16 candidates, as I just wasn't able to focus and get the interviews taped and get shows loaded to the network AND get my first magazine out. I did my best with what I had, but it was just not quite the same as 2022.

The community amongst the award recipients didn't happen. I accept fault for that, as I wasn't present enough. 2023 continued with many more challenges for my father-in-law, including a fall, a broken hip, and a move to a nursing home when rehab wasn't successful. More moving trucks later, storage units, and cleaning out a house with 60 years of contents, I spent some time in consideration of what I wanted to do moving forward. The magazine and the show continued to flourish to my delight.

I started thinking about my WOW WARRIOR honorees in November and December. Yet here I was asking myself if I should even continue with the WOW WARRIOR Award as I had completely failed (in my opinion) in 2023. I knew I would continue with the magazine and the show, but I was at a crossroads with the award portion. My husband asked me if it would matter to me if I didn't do it. I sat with that. I thought about the joy it brought me personally. I looked across my 2022 honorees. They had been working together in books, on summits, on each other's podcasts, and even joined each other in collaborative businesses.

If I removed myself and WOW WARRIOR Platform from that equation, none of those things would have been possible. I realized at that moment that I couldn't quit. If I quit, I'd have been quitting on them, myself, and my purpose. It was during that introspection that I realized when I was talking to the women about their legacy that MY legacy was intertwined in theirs. I genuinely wanted to help them succeed at a higher level, help them be seen and heard. I wanted other women to have these powerful role models to follow! I wanted to help each one of these award winners to help inspire more women. I like to say that I help you go farther faster. My legacy is helping you live out yours.

Feeling less confident than I'd like to admit, in January of 2024 I forged ahead and began the selection process. Guess what? 2024 has been a magical year full of love, kindness, collaborations and everything this award was meant to bring and more! I've been told so many times how incredibly grateful the 2024 recipients are for assembling the most amazing group of women together! As the summit and ebook are planned, I quite literally bask in the glow of these incredible women. I don't think I could have a bigger reward than seeing these women connecting and collaborating and putting good into the world!

Creating the WOW WARRIOR Platform was the BIGGEST risk of my career. I financed every part of it myself from the software to the platforms necessary to run it all, to the personnel and thousands of hours spent in development. Someone told me this past week that if I want something and it doesn't exist, I just create it.

They were right. This is exactly what I did with the WOW WARRIOR Platform. I wanted to celebrate powerful, confident women and didn't see a way to do so.

I took the biggest risk of my career and built what I needed to be able to do just that. Every day I am surrounded by the BIGGEST rewards!

Those rewards have names, and they are all WOW WARRIORS.

Sherri Leopold

Sherri Leopold, CEO of Option Creators INC, is a Mentor and Leader of the Stop Self-Bullying Movement. She is also the founder of the WOW WARRIOR Platform, publisher of WOW WARRIOR Magazine and host of the WOW WARRIOR show, and WOW- Look who's Here!

Sherri is a 12-times international bestselling author and is currently working on two upcoming books. She is currently an Ambassador Mentor Candidate and a Regional Director Candidate with Givers University.

In addition, she has over 26 years in Network Marketing/Direct Sales and experience in speaking, mentoring, and team building. She can help you transform your life mentally, physically, and financially through falling in love with yourself first.

Connect with Sherri at www.SherriLeopold.com.

CHAPTER 21

How Can Problems Plus Brain Power Equal Creativity?

Terri B Jones

To my beautiful granddaughters, Milanie and Chrisette.
May you use my 7-layer recipe to turn your problems into
purpose at every juncture in life, Love Chickee

Growing up in New Orleans, good food, fun and fellowship became the norm. It doesn't matter when or who you visit, you are bound to get a delicious bowl of gumbo. And regardless of who cooked it, you will realize that none of them are the same even though most of them use the same ingredients.

For those of us who like recreating delicious meals at home, we may end up asking the cook for the recipe. Of course, you can find recipes on how to make gumbo online and you will find all kinds of variations. For sure, this is one dish that you cannot mess up. But once you get all the ingredients, cook the dish and eat it, you end up saying something's missing. Be assured and know that when I share my gumbo recipe with you, I will not leave out any step.

The same goes for my 7-layer recipe for turning problems into purpose. I have used it over the years to position me as a product and content creator to confidently take bold risks and reap big rewards. Now that I am going to share it with you, I look forward to hearing you share your concoction of bold risks you are able to cook up resulting in big rewards.

Talking about food is probably making you hungry or, at best, curious about what's in my 7-layer recipe. Even though I have put your mind on the delicious New Orleans cuisine, let's delve into the base of my recipe which is: problems plus brain power equals creativity. And guess what? Everybody has problems whether we deal with them, ignore them or tap into our God-given creativity to solve them.

First, what is creativity? Creativity is the ability to make new things or think of new ideas. Second, what is brain power? Brain power is putting what you know into action. With this in mind, I will share with you three case studies of problems I encountered so you can envision how this 7-layer recipe can assist any problem solver with taking bold risks that result in big rewards. Third, ready to see this recipe in action? Let's take a look at how this recipe became my favorite one to use that ultimately can position you to do things you may have only imagined doing in line with your purpose here on earth.

I guess she couldn't take it anymore. "You can no longer turn in your handwritten homework; it must be typewritten," said my 8th grade

English teacher. When I asked her what the problem was, she said, "I cannot read or understand your handwriting." I knew it was a matter of time, though.

Ugly handwriting was one of the natural things I inherited from my mom. I know you might be saying to yourself, "Are you serious"? Yes, I am. Most days my mom experienced some type of stress or pressure to make ends meet to ensure we had food to eat, which I believe attributed to her ugly handwriting. So, when my teacher approached me, I understood; because I struggled to read anything my mom wrote by hand because of her handwriting. It truly was difficult, but it turned out to be the secret ingredient to my 7-layer recipe to turn that problem into purpose and generate passive income.

So how did this become the secret ingredient? I'm glad you're curious. Because of my ugly handwriting, I was able to use that problem to tap into my brain power and create six streams of income as a teenager and beyond.

I learned how to type so proficiently that my first summer job at 14 years old was as a secretary in corporate America. Not only was I great at typing, but I loved math! So, when it was time to send in the yearly income taxes to the government, it was a breeze! As the neighborhood kids found out that I was great at math and typing, they began to hire me to type their term papers and, because they had summer jobs, they also hired me to complete their income tax forms. I continued typing and completing income taxes for family and friends even after I relocated to Jacksonville, Florida. I even owned a Liberty Tax Income business franchise in 2012.

Let's fast forward to 2022. My ugly handwriting journey of learning how to type at an early age has positioned me to have almost 40 years of employment in Information Technology. I love connecting with others who also are able to use their problems as the secret recipe in their life.

As creatives, we didn't let the problems of the pandemic hinder our passion for our purpose; instead, it positioned us to extend our reach and impact.

The pandemic helped us to reach out to people around the world through online platforms such as Zoom and Facebook Lives. This collaboration empowered us to make a positive impact on our everyday lives to help deal with loneliness, anxiety and mental stresses we all were experiencing. Some people got so proficient on these platforms that they ended up achieving overnight success. Sure, I earned my share of the pot but at the same time, I was concerned with what was going on offline as well. Here's why.

After 40 years of teaching in youth ministry, I am in competition with local sports associations. Yes, you heard it right. I started teaching in youth ministry at the age of 13 and at 62 years old I still love it! I believe this is what I was put on this earth to do. Week after week, I go to church prepared to make an impact in the lives of our youth and lay a biblical foundation to let them know regardless of whether anyone tells them they are loved, Jesus loves them. Going to church is where I found love and I know that same love of Jesus is still available today. But guess what, the kids aren't coming to church! They are at a cheerleading competition or football game and basically coming to church is just not a priority anymore. This is very disheartening for me. Of course, we do have online church service, but there's nothing like seeing, hugging and touching one another in person.

Scientists say that giving another person support through touch can reduce the stress of the person being comforted. At that point, I didn't want to let it discourage me, so I began to use my 7-layer recipe and at the age of 60 in 60 days I was able to get this problem out of my head into my hands and created the Church Grower Board Game. So far, families in 12 states are experiencing positive mental health while playing this game through food, fun and fellowship.

By now I know your appetite is ready for the ingredients to my 7-layer recipe. Just like butter, flour and sugar are simple yet essential to most recipes, these 7 ingredients are simple and yet essential to my 7-layer recipe. Grab a pen and paper so you can turn your problems into purpose from here on out. Here's how I whipped up this recipe to create the Church Grower Board Game.

1. Pen and paper: Write down thoughts, inspirations, ideas. When I got the idea to create the Bible Trivia Board Game, I wrote down all the ideas that came to me.

2. Ask questions: I began to ask questions about the design of the board, the trivia question cards and the game pieces.

3. Read: Read to become an expert, spark ideas and creativity. I began searching the internet for existing board games to learn all of the things that make for a great board game.

4. Try something new: Learn how to do something you've never done before. I never saw myself creating a board game but because of my passion to make a positive impact, I took the risk and now players of this game are reaping the reward of having positive mental health through gamification.

5. Map it out: Draw pictures, write steps and instructions. This is where I used this ingredient to create a prototype of my board game.

6. Imaginary Expert Minds: Imagine experts brainstorming with you about your idea. I imagined successful board game maker Milton Bradley giving me tips and suggestions.

7. Main ingredient: Demonstrate the love of God and others in all that you do. As you include all the ingredients in line with your purpose, your dish will be the very thing your clients need, desire and want to partake of.

Was that delicious or not? I look forward to being your sous chef as you use my 7-layer recipe to turn that problem into purpose to generate passive income. I know I asked you to write down the 7-layer recipe. As a bonus, you can download the 7-layer recipe. Check my bio for download details.

Terri B Jones

Terri B Jones is the founder of Terri B Jones Live LLC. Her journey started early with a passion for technology, education and entrepreneurship.

From a teenager with six streams of income to 37 years in IT at a Fortune 500 Insurance Company, she still finds time to use her expertise in ministry, the local community and abroad as a product and content creator and financial literacy teacher.

She is an Author with 15 published books including the acclaimed *Kids Cooking Kid Friendly Kitchen Safety Tips* Book, a sought-after Speaker, Book Publisher, Online Marketer and Amazon Alexa Skills Developer.

She is the co-founder of The Life Church; TJ & TJ Insurance Agency; Jones Home Loan Mortgage with her Navy Veteran husband; Founder of Create A Prayer Pillow; creator of What the Scripture Say Day, Memorization Guide; IC2B Me Bible Trivia Tea Workshop; Can I Have Some Money Mama Youth Workshop; with her latest accomplishment during Black History Month 2022 of the Church Grower™ Board

Game used at the Bible Trivia With A Twist Events.

With the help of Terri B Jones Live LLC, you will be able to turn problems into solutions using her content creation framework. The main goal will be to create and implement actionable steps to generate exposure, traffic and visibility that lead to passive income through gamification.

Download Terri's 7-layer recipe for turning problems into purpose here https://bit.ly/tbjp7steps.

Afterword

Your Chapter Awaits

Dear Reader,

As you turn this final page, you might find yourself reflecting on the journey you've just experienced through these words. Each story you read is a tapestry of dreams, struggles, triumphs, and the relentless spirit of its creator. Now, imagine a world where your story joins these ranks – where your voice, your experiences, and your unique perspective are shared and celebrated.

This is not just an invitation; it's a call to action from Action Takers Publishing. We believe in the power of stories to transform, inspire, and connect humankind. More importantly, we believe in your story and its potential to make a significant impact on the planet.

Why wait for "someday" to tell your story? The time is now, and the world is ready to listen. Whether it's a tale of adventure, a deeply personal memoir, a groundbreaking idea, or a story that has been quietly growing in your heart, it deserves to be told.

At Action Takers Publishing, led by our Founder & CEO, Lynda Sunshine West, we specialize in turning visions into reality. We understand the journey of transforming a personal narrative into a published book – it's a journey of courage, creativity, and breaking through fears. Our team is dedicated to guiding you through every step of this exhilarating process, from the initial draft to the moment your book is held in the hands of eager readers across the globe.

Join our vibrant community of authors, a diverse group of storytellers who have dared to make their voices heard. With us, you'll find more than just a publisher; you'll discover a supportive network of mentors, editors, and fellow authors who are all committed to the success of your story.

Take the leap. Embrace the thrill of seeing your name on the cover of your very own book. Contact us at Action Takers Publishing, and let's embark on this remarkable journey together. Your story matters, and the time to share it with the world is now.

Nothing Happens Without Action.

Lynda Sunshine West
Founder & CEO
Action Takers Publishing
https://www.actiontakerspublishing.com/

p.s. Remember, every great story begins with a simple decision to start writing. Yours is no different. Let's make it happen, together.

READER BONUS!

Dear Reader,

As a thank you for your support, Action Takers Publishing would like to offer you a special reader bonus: a free download of our course, "How to Write, Publish, Market & Monetize Your Book the Fast, Fun & Easy Way." This comprehensive course is designed to provide you with the tools and knowledge you need to bring your book to life and turn it into a successful venture.

The course typically **retails for $499,** but as a valued reader, you can access it for free. To claim your free download, simply follow this link ActionTakersPublishing.com/workshops - use the discount code "coursefree" to get a 100% discount and start writing your book today.

If we are still giving away this course by the time you're reading this book, head straight over to your computer and start the course now. It's absolutely free.

READER BONUS!

ActionTakersPublishing.com/workshops
discount code "coursefree"

www.ingramcontent.com/pod-product-compliance
Lightning Source LLC
Chambersburg PA
CBHW071148120626
46546CB00006B/2176